LARGE PRINT

Lamancusa

Quilts are Forever

34305

C —
746.4
L

DATE DUE

AUG 15, 2018	

PRINTED IN U.S.A.

Quilts Are
Forever

This Large Print Book carries the
Seal of Approval of N.A.V.H.

Quilts Are Forever

A Patchwork
Collection of
Inspirational
Stories

Kathy Lamancusa

Thorndike Press • Waterville, Maine

Published in 2002 by arrangement with Simon & Schuster, Inc.

Thorndike Press Large Print Inspirational Series.

The tree indicium is a trademark of Thorndike Press.

The text of this Large Print edition is unabridged.
Other aspects of the book may vary from the original edition.

Cover design by Thorndike Press Staff.

Set in 16 pt. Plantin by Elena Picard.

Printed in the United States on permanent paper.

Library of Congress Cataloging-in-Publication Data

Lamancusa, Kathy.
    Quilts are forever : a patchwork collection of inspirational
stories / Kathy Lamancusa.
        p. cm.
    ISBN 0-7862-4355-4 (lg. print : hc : alk. paper)
    1. Quilting — Anecdotes.   I. Title.
TT835 .L28 2002b
    746.46—dc21   2002020264

*This book is dedicated to my mother,
Stella Wielicki,
who taught me to sew,*

*and to God, who guides my hand as
I stitch the quilt of life.*

Acknowledgments

The first expression of gratitude must go to the contributors who have shared their special, heartwarming stories so that others can experience the impact that quilts have on our lives. I appreciate their desire to share these moments with our readers.

My editor, Cherise Grant, at Simon & Schuster has been a true inspiration to me throughout the process of compiling this book. I love the time we have spent together over lunches and dinners in New York and Philadelphia, and have appreciated her dedication, professionalism, and most important, her spirit. Her talents pick up where mine leave off. Her guidance and direction have influenced the messages shared and will certainly have a profound impact on our readers. Cherise, you are one class act — a lady of style, grace, and spirit. I couldn't imagine doing this book without you.

Malinda Oakes, our contributor coordinator at Creative Directions, Inc., did a superb job overseeing all the small details in the compilation of these stories. I'm grateful for her editing and her talent for finding the heartfelt message in each story.

Katherine Lamancusa, my sister-in-law and business associate, has my deepest appreciation for her professionalism and dedication to the details of the project. Her ability to jump in at the last minute with a laser-sharp focus assisted in bringing this book in on deadline, for which I am eternally grateful.

My husband, Joe, helped in numerous ways from editing copy to photocopying manuscripts. I always appreciate his ability to focus and oversee the process and production. Joe, as we look forward to the second twenty-five years of our marriage, may we always sleep together under the quilt of life that we continue to stitch together.

Dr. Terry Paulson, my friend, business associate, and a lover of quilts, has been an inspiration to me throughout this process. I am grateful for his willingness to always be there when needed on the journey and help me see ways that my talents and abilities can bring hope to the lives of many. Terry, someday we *will* see *Quilters* together!

My greatest appreciation goes to God, who has allowed me to be his messenger of quilts to the world. While we often have no control over the pieces of fabric he gives us, we *can* decide into what pattern we stitch that fabric. He speaks to us through quilts, and when we listen to the message he shares, we are energized. God wants us to wrap ourselves in the quilt of life to know that he loves us and is always there for us . . . forever and ever . . . without fail . . . and unconditionally.

Contents

Chapter 1 — Sharing Special Moments

Chapter 5 — Unexpected Surprises

Introduction

The first time a quilt came into my life was during my bridal shower. My fiancé's grandmother, Nana, had spent months creating a quilt for us. It had a white background with large yellow flowers appliquéd all over it. Her fingers were swollen from the long hours she put in trying to finish the quilt on time. I felt bad, but I was so excited about the quilt. Yellow was my favorite color, and this handmade treasure was breathtaking! As soon as Joe and I got married, this quilt took residence on our bed and stayed there, bringing us comfort and warmth for many years.

When my son, Joey, was born two years later, a second quilt from Nana appeared out of a beautifully wrapped box at his baby shower. This one was blue with appliquéd circles and diamonds. Joey was born at the very start of the worst blizzard in history, so he and I couldn't leave the hospital for five days. Once my husband went home after the birth, he couldn't get back to the hospital for several days due to the extreme weather. When Joe was finally able to bring us home, I wrapped Joey in the quilt his great-grandmother had made for him. As he grew, Joey would wrap himself in it and carry it with him around the house. It continued to be his companion until he started school.

When I was growing up, my mother and I made blouses, skirts, slacks, and dresses. I even sewed a few pillows. But we never stitched anything that was particularly intricate, so these quilts had a big impact on me. I was intrigued by their beautiful design, color, and pattern. I was warmed by their touch and feel. I found they comforted me. But after seeing the swollen state of Nana's fingers, and finding little time to myself with two small sons, I had no desire to jump in and hand stitch a quilt of my own.

Several years later as I was browsing in a fabric store, I ran across a new technique for creating a quilt by sewing machine instead of by hand, which promised that you could make a quilt in one day. We had just built a home, and I thought a new bedspread would be nice. Believing the advertising, I bought all the fabric and instructions needed. Once I got started, I never could figure out how to make a "quilt in a day." The quilt top alone took me several months. Once finished with the top I became frustrated with the whole process and the quilt went into a closet, where it stayed for five years.

One day when cleaning that closet, I retrieved the quilt top and thought, "Well, now, I should probably finish that," and I placed it on my sewing machine table, where it sat for several more years. Looking at it day after day made me feel guilty, and when I couldn't stand it any longer, I vowed another weekend would not pass with this unfinished quilt sitting by my sewing machine. So I made sure there was enough food to feed the family for three days, closed the door to the basement, where my sewing machine was, and didn't quit (except to sleep for a few hours and eat enough to sustain me) until the quilt was finished! It has been on our bed ever since.

While I may never have the time or patience to sew a complete quilt by hand, I certainly do admire every person who does. What I learned, though, was that it doesn't matter whether the quilt is hand or machine stitched, it is the commitment of your time and energy that infuses the love, and it is the love that speaks to us each time we wrap ourselves in it, creating the language of the quilt.

After I finished that first quilt, I began to make more. They never took me as long as that first one, and each quilt I designed was created specifically for someone I loved. Immersing myself in the colors and motifs of the fabrics and the beauty of various pattern designs was refreshing, and I found myself spending more and more time creating quilts. I couldn't help but notice how my sons loved my quilts: my younger son, Jimmy, wrapped tightly in his brightly colored dinosaur quilt watching television when he wasn't feeling well, and my older son, Joey, helping me design a quilt during his recovery from a near-fatal automobile accident while our family was in England.

I found that I wasn't alone in appreciating the language of quilts. In this book, you'll get to meet quilt makers, quilt recipients, and quilt lovers who feel the same. Their stories will show you how the fabric of life is much like the fabric in quilts. We stitch together individual moments of time like we stitch together pieces of fabric. Some of the moments are so dark and depressing, we wouldn't have selected them to be a part of our life quilt if we had the choice. However, every quilt aficionado knows that a successful design must be a balance of dark and light fabrics. The dark provides the contrast and helps the light fabrics become visually compelling. Isn't it interesting that mere remnants, scraps, and discarded clothing can be sewn together to create a work of art that comforts and connects?

Mary White, a Texas quilter from the 1900s, may have said it best:

You can't always change things. Sometimes you don't have no control over the way things go. Hail ruins the crops, or fire burns you out. And then you're just given so much to work with in a life and you have to do the best you can with what you've got. That's what piecing is. The material is passed on to you or is all you can afford to buy . . . that's just what's given to you. Your fate. But the way you put them together is your business. You can put them in any order you like.

May these stories inspire you and bring you comfort and joy as they have me. I hope you take the time to look at your life a little differently after you read them. Please share these stories with those you love most in the world.

CHAPTER 1

Sharing Special Moments

*Friendships
are sewn . . .
one stitch at
a time.*

The Double-Wedding Ring Quilt

BRENDA DIAL

My local quilt guild was displaying quilts at a heritage festival. As part of the festival, visitors were able to tour dozens of restored buildings. My guild was displaying and conducting quilting demonstrations in one of the smaller buildings.

I was making my way across the courtyard area, talking to friends and checking out the other crafts on display. And then someone called my name. As I turned to look at the person, I caught a quilt out of the corner of my eye. A king-sized, double-wedding ring quilt hung from the second-floor, outer railing of the old house. The gentle breeze ruffled the edges slightly. Maybe it was the colors moving in the breeze. I don't know for sure, but I stopped moving and stared up at it.

25

It took me a moment to realize that the quilt was actually mine. I had only seen it while I was sewing on the small pieces, while I was quilting on it in a small lap frame, or while it was lying on top of a bed. I had never seen it from a distance and I had never seen it fully laid out. From the distance, you couldn't see the coffee stain or the frayed corner. All you could see was the beautiful maroon fabrics shining against the muslin. For that instant, I was alone. It seemed as if no one else existed in the entire universe. While staring at the quilt, I was flooded with memories.

I had started the quilt while my grandmother was dying of cancer in the hospital. During the long days spent at her bedside, I passed the time by cutting the numerous tiny pieces needed for the quilt. Even though most of the time my grandmother didn't know I was there, I stayed with her because it was important to me. She was important to me. During those same weeks I learned that I was pregnant with my third child. It was a bittersweet realization that my new child would never know the woman I was sitting with. My unborn daughter and I were sharing the few moments I had left with my grandmother, yet she would never hear her great-grandmother's laugh or listen as she told a story.

I began sewing the pieces together at about the same time that I felt my daughter move for the first time. My grandmother died soon thereafter, and the quilt was put away for a few months as other things took precedence — preparing for the new arrival, taking care of the two children I already had.

Later in the pregnancy, I took up the sewing project again. I began sewing on the top just before the C-section that delivered my baby. I was still working on it when we took the thousand-mile journey by car to visit my husband's family to introduce them to the newborn. The tiny pieces of fabric dropped between the seats or underfoot as I moved to stop arguments between my other two small children, pass out drinks or snacks, and nurse our new baby. I had to cut more than a hundred extra pieces to make up for the losses from that trip.

Back at home, I quilted at night after the kids went to bed. It was a bit of sanity in the middle of my otherwise chaotic life. I bundled the quilt onto my lap during cold evenings as my husband worked nights. I snuggled a sleeping little one beside me when one of them woke up and I wanted to keep quilting. It became therapeutic to work on it when I became pregnant twice more and lost both babies.

It wasn't until the quilt was almost finished that I found a massive hole all the way through it. I still cringe at the memory. My son had spilled some hydrogen peroxide on it and failed to tell me. He was afraid that I would be upset. My son was right: I was mad. The hydrogen peroxide had eaten through the top, batting, backing, and quilting stitches. I had to unstitch the adjoining pieces and inset replacement material. Then I had to re-quilt the area, trying to make everything match up. Now, as I look back, with so much time having passed, I chuckle to myself as I remember.

Finally, two years after I had first started cutting the pieces, I was finished. I gave the huge creation to my mother for Christmas. My mother ran into her bedroom, with the quilt hugged against her, and gently placed the king-sized quilt on top of her queen-sized bed. It was too large for the bed and hung almost to the floor, but she wouldn't think of tucking it under the mattress, folding it to leave on a shelf, or hanging it for display. It was her quilt and she was going to use it!

I continued to stare up at the quilt on the railing as I remembered taking my sister's sleeping new baby daughter and laying her on top of the quilt. I stood there watching her as she slept. She was so beautiful. I cried on top of it, a short time later, when I shared with my mother that I couldn't have any more children.

I remembered other times when I had played with the kids, mine as well as nieces and nephews, on top of it. There were times when we cuddled together beneath it on holidays as we watched television. It was big enough to cover all of us at once. I've laid on it while discussing plans and dreams with my mother and sister, and I've wrapped Christmas presents on top of it.

All of those memories and more flooded my mind as I looked across the open space to the softly flowing fabric of the prized creation. Tears welled in my eyes and my throat tightened as I tried not to cry. I would have succumbed to the emotions if my friend, the one who had called my name, had not reached out and touched my arm.

The noise and the movement around me in the crowded yard rushed me back to the present. It was a bit disorienting. I had to look around to remind myself where I was.

"Is that your quilt?" she asked, pointing toward my quilt.

I nodded. I didn't trust myself to speak just yet.

"Is it new? I don't think I've ever seen it here before."

"No, it's not new. It's sort of been in the family a while." I shrugged. I wasn't going to go into the full story. I didn't want to admit how many years that quilt had survived.

"Wow! Well, make sure you take care of it. You wouldn't want the kids to get hold of that one. It's a masterpiece."

I smiled, thanked her, and looked back at the quilt as she walked off. The maroons were as dark as ever, the muslin as pale. The small flaws in my stitching didn't show and neither did the inserted pieces. I didn't have the words to tell her that kids, family, and friends are the very things that made my quilt special. She just wouldn't have understood.

A quilt consists of three layers: a quilt top, a filling material or batting, and a backing. The three layers are held together or "quilted" using a basic running stitch done by hand or sewing machine. Stitching yarn or narrow ribbon can also be used, working them through the layers at regular intervals and tying off the ends to hold the layers in place. The goal is to keep the layers from shifting.

■ ■ ■

■ *Quilting became widely popular in America during the second half of the eighteenth century as leisure time and the abundance of imported materials became available. Women spent many hours creating elaborately pieced and appliquéd quilts. The ability to sew and fine needlework skills gave testimony to good breeding. Their fashions and lifestyle were significantly influenced by European society and the methods and styles of England. Quilts made during this time, now preserved in museums, were made from European fabric and clearly reflect the English style.*

Too Cool for a Quilt

JOE LAMANCUSA, JR.

When you're eighteen years old, heading into your freshman year of college, the last thing you want is for your mom to make you a quilt to put on your dorm room bed. Just imagine the ridicule that one would derive from sleeping under a homespun bedspread. "Mama's boy!" "Blankie Baby!"

But that's exactly what my mom wanted to do. Thoughts of sending her oldest child off to school for the first time left her with all kinds of feelings of separation that she didn't want to face. She took her job of being a mother very seriously, and since I had loved the quilt she made me for my bed at home, she was determined to make me a quilt for my bed at school so I wouldn't feel lonely. Her intentions were good enough, but what she didn't realize was that I had no intentions of being lonely. Hey, I was going to be a college kid! Yahoo!

But Mom couldn't put aside her motherly instincts. She just wanted to be sure that her "baby boy" would be warm during the long, cold nights in an unfamiliar dorm. She wanted to have a little piece of herself there with me since she couldn't be there. She wanted to give me a long-distance hug every night as I went to bed. Blah, blah, blah. In reality, secretly I wanted all those things, too. I *was* really going to miss my mom. But familial affection takes a back seat to being cool in front of your friends when you're eighteen and on your way out to see the world.

So I told my mom, "Thanks, but no thanks." I figured I'd just get a neutral bedspread at the co-op when I got to school. Something benign and unassuming. Something that wouldn't attract any attention or solicit any ridicule. I didn't want to make a bad impression on my roommate and my neighbors in the dorm before they even talked to me. *Surely* my mom would understand.

She didn't. She kept asking and asking, assuring me that she could create a cool quilt that would place me in an elite position among my new friends. "Hey look, there's Joe! He's the one with that awesome quilt on his bed. I want to be his friend!" Yeah right, Mom. You don't know how college kids are.

But she kept asking . . . and asking. Finally, I relented.

"Alright," I said. "We'll go look at fabrics *together* and if, *if* we find a pattern that I can live with, you can make me a quilt."

The shakeout at the fabric store was brutal. I was on edge and would instantly veto anything that looked even remotely uncool.

"Too girly, Mom."

"Nope, that one's too flowery."

"I can't sleep under butterflies!"

Flustered and frustrated, my mom frantically looked around for anything that would appease my impossible judgment.

"What about this?" she asked, holding up an interesting pattern of abstract paint bursts on a rich blue background. I turned around, ready to give my indictment, and was pleasantly surprised. It definitely wasn't girly. There were no flowers on it. It was kind of . . . um . . . cool. As soon as I hesitated, my mom knew that she had me. I mulled it over, comparing the pattern to all the other cool bedspreads I had seen in the freshman catalogs that arrived daily in the mail. Yeah, I think I can live with this one.

"OK," I said. "But no cross-stitching in the middle," trying to save a little face.

Mom did as she promised — she made me a cool bedspread that was safe from teasing. She didn't even put any wimpy "mommy" embellishments on it . . . except one. On the inside edge where no one else could see it, she pinned a guardian angel secured with a little dab of silicone glue so it wouldn't come off in a night of fitful sleep. Next to the angel she wrote: "Dear Joe, For you . . . a quilt to keep you warm and an angel to keep you safe . . . all my love, Mom."

During my four years of school, Mom's quilt kept me warm and spoke to me of her love. Not only did I not get teased, it turned out to be a great conversation starter! I found others were even jealous that their relationship with their moms didn't include something as special as a handmade quilt. And even though I was *too cool* for it, I was thankful to have that guardian angel close to me, and I looked forward to a warm "Mom" hug every night.

■ *A quilt should never be hung over a clothes-line to dry. The extra water weight may cause the quilt to lose its shape or even pop some quilting stitches. Press excess water out of the quilt and then lay it out flat on a clean sheet outdoors in the shade on a warm day to dry. Avoid direct sunlight. A clean sheet can be placed on top to protect it from birds and any other airborne materials. To dry indoors, place a sheet over a carpet. Run a fan close by to keep air circulating.*

■ *Friendship quilts involve the participation of many. They are often made of scraps and varying patterns, and each quilter usually signs a block. The quilts are used to commemo-rate a birthday, wedding, anniversary, retire-ment, or other milestone event. Many times they are used as a gift to someone who is moving away, with each quilt block containing a friend's name and mailing address.*

Going Back in Time

Patricia Laderer

It seemed as though I went back in time when I moved to Wren, Mississippi. The year was 1977, but it felt more like 1957. Shortly after my arrival, I was invited to join the West Wren Culture Club, which was a social group that met in members' homes. I was a young mother trying to understand the local dialect and make a few friends. The meetings reminded me of the Home Bureau meetings my mother had in our home when I was growing up — the conversation would be filled with homemaker's tips, the latest decorating ideas, and information on when the next quilting bee would be held.

I had never been to a quilting bee before, but fondly remember a blue-and-white quilt my mother had made years ago. Perhaps now was the time to start quilting. I was anxious to learn the craft.

Miss Eva Mae, a member of the club, invited me to her house for my first quilting bee. She was seventy-five or eighty years old and lived "next door," which meant about a quarter mile down the highway. Explaining how a quilting bee worked, she said the hostess of the bee makes a quilt top. Once it's finished, her friends and family attend to help her stitch the top, batting, and backing together to make a complete quilt. Each woman would bring a food dish for a potluck dinner they would eat at noon. We would quilt all morning, eat a huge meal, and then quilt all afternoon. I was so excited to be going to a real quilting bee. This was history come alive!

The big day arrived. Miss Eva Mae had her quilt all assembled on a frame in the front room, her unused parlor. The quilt frame was four one-by-twos clamped together at the corners with C clamps. Chairs rested under each corner to hold it up. The quilt consisted of the bottom layer, which was a king-sized sheet tacked to the frame, a middle layer of quilt batting, and the top layer, which was fabric with a pattern of appliquéd irises and leaves. The three layers had already been basted together. The frame took up the whole room. There were twelve chairs around the frame, four each on the long sides and two each on the short ends.

"Come set here, Pat," Miss Eva Mae invited.

"I've never quilted before. What do you do?" I replied.

"It's easy. Here's a needle and some thread; tie a knot," she said, and that was the beginning of my lesson.

After stitching a while I looked over at Miss Laura's stitches and saw how tiny and neat they were. I watched as she poked the needle straight down through the layers and came up again close to the first stitch. Using a thimble, she poked the needle down and up again and again. She made it look so easy, but to my dismay I discovered that it was not all that easy. As hard as I tried, my stitches were still twice as big as Miss Laura's.

"Are you sure you want me to do this? My stitches aren't very little," I asked.

"As long as your big toe won't catch the thread, it's small enough," she chuckled.

Around the quilt frame, the ladies were reaching as far as they could, stitching toward the middle. As sections of the quilt were stitched, the women unclamped and rolled the quilt on the frame, making it smaller. By noon, the quilt was quite a bit narrower than it had started out. Miss Eva Mae and her friend Miss Jewell went into the kitchen to start setting out the food.

"Come on, y'all, dinner's ready." The rest of us wandered into the dining room to a table as full as some Thanksgiving tables that I've seen. There was turkey, cornbread dressing, gravy, green beans, pinto beans, peas, butter beans, fried okra, all kinds of pickles, mashed potatoes, baked sweet potatoes, and an assortment of desserts that would put any five-star restaurant to shame.

Conversation was lively while we ate. It revolved around the soybean harvest, the next quilting bee, and local gossip.

After eating we were so full that we waddled back into the front room to quilt some more. Everyone was ready for a good nap after lunch, so the afternoon's progress went a bit slower. Along about 3:30, various women began to leave to get home in time for kids or grandkids. Several promised to come back in the morning to finish.

Before I left, Miss Eva Mae showed me the quilt on her bed. The pattern was called "Around the World" and was made with four-by-four-inch squares positioned in rows of colors. It looked so simple to make, yet was so beautiful. I decided to make one for my daughter using the scraps I already had. I hurried home, excited by the whole idea of making my own quilt.

While I assembled the top, I continued to attend other quilting bees, learning more each time and meeting friends who would help me when my time came.

The big day for my own quilting bee finally arrived. I borrowed Miss Eva Mae's frame and had it set up in my living room. It was spring and fewer of the women were available to come because it was planting time, but those who came worked hard. We got a lot done and, of course, ate well. Since there were fewer hands to help during the quilting bee, it took me several more weeks to finish the quilt.

After stepping back to admire the finished work, I reflected on the beauty of the quilt, but more important on what quilting bees had done for me. They provided a way for me to integrate my life into the community, providing the ability to deepen my relationships with the other women. I truly felt accepted by this old-fashioned community and knew that we would all stick together through good times and bad.

Because of that first invitation from Miss

Eva Mae, the quilting bug has bitten and I have since made quilts for my nephew's wedding, my grandniece and two grandnephews, my grandson, and of course, for myself. All have been made with the help of friends and family. As time moves forward, I plan to keep making quilts . . . and friends.

■ *It is best to store your quilts flat on a spare bed. Not everyone has enough room to do this, so if quilts are stored folded, refold them several times a year to eliminate permanent creases.*

■ *When giving a quilt as a gift, wrap it in acid-free tissue paper and include instructions for storing it safely.*

■ *Use a small amount of hydrogen peroxide or saliva to remove blood spots on the fabric from pricked fingers. Saliva contains an enzyme that will decolorize blood and remove fresh bloodstains.*

■ *After completing a quilt, place the pattern instruction sheets in a clear plastic page protector along with scraps of the fabrics used. Note when the quilt was finished and other pertinent information such as how many hours or months were spent on completing the project. Keep these plastic pages in a binder to create a record of all your quilt projects.*

A Broken Cup

SUZANN THOMPSON

My two-year-old daughter, Eva, wanted to snack on raisins. We couldn't find any of the usual plastic or metal bowls we usually use, so I decided to put them into a pretty china cup with a rose pattern that I had bought twenty years before on a visit to my grandmother in Germany. "Be careful, because I really like this cup," I said.

Eva has always been a careful girl, and she carried the cup without incident into the living room so she could sit with her dad. For a little while I heard them talking, but then I heard loud crying and intuitively knew that my cup was broken.

I questioned whether I should have loaned such a sentimental treasure to a two-year-old. I picked up the pieces but couldn't bring myself to throw them away.

44

The shards lay in a cupboard for a couple of years. I thought of them often and each time I did, some important questions came to mind:

- *Which is more important — a pretty cup or a happy child?*
- *Should we teach children of all ages to enjoy beauty and to take care of beautiful things?*
- *Are we willing to accept the consequences?*
- *Is it so important to have things to remind us of certain times in our lives?*
- *Do we need to shed sentimental things in order to move on with our lives?*

As I thought about the questions, the answers were clear to me. I would choose a happy child over a pretty cup every time. You are never too young to see and enjoy beautiful things. I felt sure that even young children can learn to take care of things, within reason.

I wasn't so sure about letting go of sentimental treasures. The objects we hold dear mark our passage through life. They say something about where we've been and what we've done. In a way, they are memories we can hold in our hands.

The teenage girl who bought that pretty rose cup has grown up and changed in many ways, but parts of her are still a part of me. Instead of getting rid of our sentimental things, we might just rearrange them from time to time to reflect our creative, spiritual, and mental growth and the changes we undergo as we get older.

These thoughts led to the creation of a quilt that I named "Shards Two: Sometimes." I made a fabric copy of the cup, which became a vase filled with fabric flowers in the quilt. I glued eye pins to the back of each piece of broken china, covered the back and sides of the pieces with polymer clay, baked to cure the clay, and then sewed pieces of the real cup to the quilt through the eye pins. They represent the conclusion I came to after many months of thought: "Sometimes a good thing must be broken before we can make another, better thing." In fact, I think quilts in general demonstrate this truth. We must cut up perfectly good yards of fabric into pieces in order to make a quilt, which when sewn together is more lovely, more special, and more valuable.

Since it was finished, I came to see "Shards Two" as the story of the relationship between my daughter and me. From the beginning, we've been breaking things, like assumptions (mostly mine!). Some breaks are difficult, like the one that oc-curred when she started school. Some are simple, like the cup and several other pieces of china, which we now collect for a future mosaic-making session.

So far we have been able to take the best of the broken pieces and forge them into a better and stronger relationship. I hope we will continue the cycle of constructive breaking down and building up all through our lives. No foolish assumption, no unrea-sonable expectation, and certainly no sen-timental cup will ever be as important to me as she is.

■ *Choose a washable, puffy batting for quilts that will be used frequently and require washing care. Use a thinner batting for a quilt that will be used only for display or for hanging on a wall.*

■ *Thin batting gives a quilt an older, antique look. It is easier to make smaller quilt stitches with thin batting.*

■ *Fluff batting in the dryer for a few minutes to increase its volume and smooth it out.*

■ *Many quilters favor polyester batting because it doesn't shrink or shift during laundering and use.*

■ *Batting may be "glazed" by the manufacturer. This means it has been coated with a light resin to keep the fibers from bearding and losing fibers through the quilt top. The resin coating also helps the needle to penetrate more easily.*

■ *Unwrap or unfold batting a few days before using. This gives it a chance to "breathe," expand, and relax after being packaged and stored.*

To Be Remembered

BRENDA BULLOCK

In the mid- to late forties, my grandparents lived on the corner of a busy intersection in Los Angeles, California. Notorious for fatal accidents, the corner was a constant source of distress to my tenderhearted grandmother.

One afternoon, the unmistakable sounds of a crash drew my grandmother from her house to find a child lying nearly on her doorstep. Her natural instincts sent her back into the house to find something to cover and comfort the critically injured little boy. The first thing her hand found was the quilt my mother had made, which was spread over her bed. Without a second thought, she grabbed it and tenderly covered him. Grandmother watched as the child, wrapped in the quilt, was loaded into the ambulance, never to hear from him again. The quilt went with him and was never returned.

Two years after this accident, I was born. As a single mom, Mother found it difficult to support and care for me on her own, so my grandparents became my caregivers. When I was about four, Mother married a navy man. Wanting a more stable environment for me, my mother allowed me to live with and be raised by my grandparents.

The sixties found my sailor stepfather stationed on a ship in the war-torn waters off Vietnam. Like many military wives of that era, Mother spent many sleepless nights walking the floor and praying for his safety and return. Her thoughts turned to the quilt, lost so many years ago. During this time of disquiet and constant worry, thoughts of the quilt seemed to be a point of concentration that relieved her worries and drained some of her anxiety. She asked my grandmother for the pattern so she could re-create the old quilt, but my grandma discovered that the pattern was lost. Mother searched and inquired, but was never able to find the unusual pattern. Having only her memory to guide her, after days and nights of sketching and ex-perimental piecing, she finally had a draft of the pattern, as well as a handful of blocks.

During this same time, my grandmother's health was failing. Mother was an able seamstress and could sew blocks together, but she was not a quilter. She sent the newly drawn draft and pieced blocks off to Grandma, believing that the chance to stitch this quilt, re-creating the one from long ago, might help my grandmother regain some much-needed energy and optimism. When Grandma opened the package, she was cheered as she thought of how much the quilt must have meant to my mother for her to take the time to re-create it in this way. However, with her vision having deteriorated, Grandma could no longer do the tedious work needed to quilt. The blocks and draft were carefully stored away, along with Grandma's other partially finished quilt projects, and sadly, forgotten.

My grandmother died in the early eighties. I was enlisted to go through her keepsakes and dispense with some items, but family photos, the stacks of crocheted items, embroidery work, and quilt blocks were too dear to lose, so they went home with me.

Over the years of my childhood, the

51

miles put between my mother and step-father and me caused an estrangement be-tween us that was unavoidable. Years later, after I married and had children of my own, everyone wanted to reconnect and make up for lost time together. Mother and I took difficult steps toward building a bridge in our relationship. In 1990, Mother and my stepfather came to visit me in Arkansas from her home in California. Trying to find common ground, I took out Grandma's treasured handwork. Each item stirred memories in us and we began to share those memories with each other. We marveled at the incredible skill and talent of the woman we both still deeply missed. When Mother saw the unusual quilt blocks, she became very quiet. With tears in her eyes, she told me the story of how these blocks had gotten into Grandma's stack of unfinished projects.

She explained to me the challenges she faced so many years ago as she tried to re-create the blocks. She remembered the quilt from her childhood as a "bed full of open umbrellas that were pieced together like a string quilt on paper." It was difficult to understand her description, but I began to sketch the words into a picture on paper. Though I've never seen the original quilt, it seems as real and familiar to me as the faces of my family.

Grandma and Mother accepted the fact that the original quilt was lost forever — or was it? Although it was lost nearly sixty years ago, thoughts of this quilt continue to materialize, providing comfort and warmth during times of distress and need. Although the quilt was sacrificed to a hurt and suffering child, I believe it returns, in its own way, time after time. When my mother desperately needed a point of focus to preserve sanity, this quilt brought positive diversion. It provided hope for my grandmother when she felt life no longer held anything but pain and loss. Thirty years later, it helped bridge a chasm carved between two women, who although mother and daughter, had been little more than strangers for most of their lives.

Now my children are adults and I have a delightful granddaughter of my own. Perhaps one day I'll re-create this beautiful quilt, allowing it to comfort and cheer in generations to come. Then again, perhaps I don't need to. It seems to find its own place in our lives, and maybe that is enough.

■ *The difference between a "template" and a "pattern" is that a template is cut from stiff, sturdy materials like plastic (clear is best), old file folders, heavy card stock, or cardboard. A pattern is printed on paper or fabric.*

A template provides a more solid surface to trace around. It is a better choice when making multiple blocks because paper is flimsy and will deteriorate quickly when handled frequently.

Templates can be made from a variety of sources:
- ■ *Washed sheets of plastic that come in bacon packages*
- ■ *Recycled plastic place mats*
- ■ *The flat area of a gallon bottle of water, large vinegar jug, bleach bottle, or milk jug*
- ■ *Plastic lids from coffee cans or ice cream containers*
- ■ *Acetate sheet protectors from discarded reports and papers*

The Patchwork Footstool

Reneé Sparks

It was just before dawn on that Sunday morning in June 1924 when Erven Harris secretly eased the horse and buggy onto the dirt road and turned toward the preacher's house several miles away. Beside him on the buggy seat sat his soon-to-be bride, Lucille Harper. She was the oldest of ten children and her father's pride and joy, but they were eloping with no warning. Erven was seventeen and Lucille was fifteen. Their families wouldn't have given permission for a union this young.

To their surprise, before they reached the preacher's home, they met him on the road. He was walking and thinking about the sermon that he would give in a few hours to the congregation. Erven stopped the buggy and told him that he and Lucille wanted to be married. The preacher was quiet for a long moment. Then he looked up at them and said, "Well, get out of the buggy." They climbed down and were married right there, in the middle of the dirt road, with the dew from the grassy pastures glistening on each side. For the next fifty-three years they lived happily married and were the best grandparents a kid could ever hope for.

They started with nothing, but through hard work and a deep faith in God, they eventually had a forty-acre farm on Sand Mountain in Alabama. The work never seemed to end as, from dawn to dusk, they raised cotton, bell peppers, chickens, and three fine sons — Chalmer (my dad), Korl, and Wymer.

Over the years, my grandfather developed bad knees — probably from climbing up and down to get on and off his tractor so often — so he wanted a good footstool to rest his legs on at night. As always, he had to make do — or do without — so he made one himself. This wasn't just any footstool. This one was here for life! He made it of two-by-fours and it was a foot and a half tall by two feet wide with plywood sides that went almost to the floor. It must have weighed fifty pounds!

After building it, he turned it over to Grandmother to cover it. He thought a quilted cover would be nice.

Grandma learned to quilt at a very young age from her mother. With only fireplaces for heat, quilts were not made merely to be pretty, but were a necessity for keeping warm. She had saved all the old wool clothes she could, thinking they would make an especially warm quilt for those long winter nights, but knowing that a footstool would need a sturdy cover, she used some of these to make the covering. She cut rectangular pieces and sewed them together on her old sewing machine. Even though they were already bright and colorful, she embroidered each seam in golden yellow yarn using a briar stitch. She covered the stool with batting, then with the beautiful quilted top. She secured the corners with brass tacks. Granddaddy loved it. Every night after supper he would sit in his rocker, prop up his tired knees, and rest.

When my mom and dad married in 1951, they moved to Marietta, Georgia, where Dad had a job with the newly opened Lockheed Aircraft Corporation. No two people had ever been so homesick. With only enough money to go home to

Alabama once a month, they started a routine that they kept up for more than thirty years. As we children were born, we joined them on their monthly visits. To them it may have been the family home, but to my two brothers, my sister, and me it was paradise. We were in country heaven. It had a big white barn to romp in, a pond to fish in, and enough dirt to go barefoot in to our hearts' content.

In the evening, everyone would gather in the den and sit in front of the big stone fireplace after supper. We talked and laughed, popped popcorn, and watched television. When my grandfather decided it was time, he stood up, turned off the TV, and said, "It's time to hit the hay." Without being told, we all knelt where we were. Grandmother knelt beside Granddaddy, both leaning on the patchwork-quilted footstool. Our heads bowed, we prayed silently while Grandmother and Granddaddy prayed aloud. I can still hear their voices as they took turns and prayed for the sick and shut-ins, for the servicemen overseas so far from home. They prayed for the preacher and his family, thanked God for the rain we had gotten that day, for the good crop he had blessed them with, and much more. Grandmother always finished before Granddaddy and as he continued she would say, "Yes, thank you, Lord." When he finished, there was a moment of silence, then an "Amen" and everyone went off to bed. This was the routine they followed every night for their entire lives. It never wavered. It never changed.

I was much older before I realized that not all families did this. Now, as an adult, my grandparents in heaven, I realize how much I miss those trips. To see the faith and trust they had in the Lord day in and day out — through good times and bad — was a great example to the entire family. What a sweet, wonderful legacy they left us! It makes me wonder how different all our lives would be if everyone had a patchwork-quilted footstool.

Album quilts, also called friendship quilts, were used to record friendships and experiences. The design features inked signatures and sentiments, like those found in a bound autograph album book.

Quilt blocks used to create early designs were sometimes called "beggar's blocks" because friends were asked not only for a souvenir of their dress, but for their signature as well.

■ ■ ■

■ *Crazy quilts, a style popular in the late nineteenth century, use fancy patchwork designs that incorporate silk and velvet fabrics along with embroidery.*

■ *A popular quilt for beginners is the sampler quilt. The design incorporates quilt blocks of all different patterns.*

■ *Scrap quilts can use several dozen or even several hundred different fabrics. Fabrics can be old or new.*

Necessity or Passion?

JOSEPHINE MCCLOUD ORETO

The making of quilts was a necessity during my childhood because there was no electricity to keep us warm. My family and I lived in a tenant farmhouse that was sealed so poorly that the wallpaper sometimes fluttered in the wind. Our only sources of heat were a fireplace in the living room and a cookstove in the kitchen. Sometimes the nights would be so cold that we needed five or six quilts on each bed to provide enough warmth for sleeping. My mother, Lucretia Tucker McCloud, spent many hours cutting and stitching those quilts for our family.

One of my earliest memories is of Mama's wooden quilting frame. It hung from ropes attached to hooks in the ceiling in the living room of our Tennessee home, taking up most of the living space in our tiny home. Mama's needle would fly, hour after hour, through the layers of material and cotton batting. She spent the lonely, wintry days completing one quilt after another. At night, Mama would roll the framed quilt she was working on all the way up to the ceiling to get it out of the way. Then we could sit around the fireplace where the logs crackled in the flames. As we huddled close to the fire, we read by the light of a coal oil lamp.

Mama would sometimes quilt for others at seventy-five cents per quilt top, a far cry from what it costs today! In those days, quilting was a skill every girl was supposed to learn. How else would her future family stay warm without the quilts she would someday sew? So Mama taught us to quilt. She'd let us practice our quilting stitches by using a threaded needle without knotting the end of the thread, so she could pull the stitches out later.

Mama hand pieced her last quilt top at age ninety-five. Today I use that quilt as a cover for my dining room table. She is now 105 years old and still attending the same church that she did when she was thirteen. Her eyesight dimming, she sorely misses her former favorite pastime — quilting — but her love ran so deep and her passion was so contagious that she inspired three of her daughters to continue the tradition of quilting. These days, though, the quilting isn't done out of necessity but with pure passion.

There are a multitude of products available to protect and prolong the life of a treasured quilt. Many can be found in spray form that will protect fabrics from stains and moisture, by repelling dirt and liquid spills. Some even strengthen the fibers for longer wear. Others are available to protect quilts and textiles from ultraviolet light to retard fading. Always follow manufacturers' instructions for application and curing times.

■ ■ ■

Sunshine and Shadows

FRANKIE WOLGAMOTT

The year 1944 was one of emotional upheaval for Fannie Wolgamott, the woman who would later become my mother-in-law. That year she would say different good-byes to her husband and her only two children. At the young age of eighteen, her sons, Melvin, whom I later married, and his twin brother, Clarence, were drafted into the army. Their father died suddenly of a stroke only a few months later, and after his funeral, these young twins were sent to Germany.

Knowing the agony Fannie must be feeling, Ina Ledford, one of her friends, thought it would be helpful if Fannie had something to keep her mind occupied rather than having only to wait and pray for her sons' safe return. At Ina's suggestion, Fannie distributed patterns to neighbor ladies who would participate in making friendship quilts for her sons. Working on this project gave Fannie a feeling that she was doing something of value for her boys and it helped her get through this very uncertain time.

When Melvin and I got married a few months after his discharge, she gave us one of the quilts as a wedding gift. So began the enrichment that handwork would bring to our marriage. Melvin loved all kinds of handwork and throughout our marriage, every room in our home, in some way, evidenced that love.

Over time, he developed emphysema, and by the time we were forty-five years into our marriage, Melvin had to be on oxygen all the time. He found himself unable to do the handwork that he loved so much and we began to realize that our time together was limited.

One day I was cutting pieces for a quilt and I noticed that he looked quite depressed. Hoping to redirect his focus from what seemed inevitable, I showed him how to use the rotary cutter. I just let him keep cutting, never telling him when to stop. After he cut more cloth than was needed for the quilt, it was time for him to learn to use the sewing machine. He used the

Singer Featherweight machine and I used my heavier machine on the dining table.

By this time, his confidence had built enough that he felt ready to tackle a larger project — and it was a big one. He planned to make six log cabin quilt tops for his six granddaughters. He went to work and planned to finish them before Christmas. He finished them on time, and it gave him such a great sense of accomplishment that he didn't stop! He continued and made several other quilt tops. He was unable to finish the last top he started because of a growth on his optic nerve. It was a quilt pattern fittingly called "Sunshine and Shadows."

Now, six years after his death, I have finished it. Today I can still walk through our house and be reminded of him in every room. His handiwork is everywhere. All are reminders of the life we shared together, but the quilts, especially the one he was unable to finish, speak to me most.

As I look at our wedding gift from his mother — now fifty-six years later — I can clearly understand the comfort she received. As she prayed for the safe return of her twin boys, the quilting project became a positive focus, taking her mind away from the agony of waiting. Sharing the project with friends provided much-needed companionship during such a painful time. Though many years had passed, another good-bye waiting, quilting again provided comfort — this time for Melvin and me in our time of uncertainty. It enabled a man who felt discouraged to experience the last days of his life that were filled with purpose and a sense of great accomplishment. For me, it provided cherished, unforgettable time and companionship with the man I loved.

■ *Cut thread on an angle. Try needling the thread instead of threading the needle. Sometimes wetting the needle instead of the thread helps.*

■ *Thread from twelve to twenty needles before you start your quilting so you don't have to stop. Do this early in the day when you see more clearly.*

■ *Kinks, tangles, fraying, and knots may form in threads while working on a quilt project. There are a variety of conditioners available made especially for thread that can be used to coat it with a layer of silicone to prevent snarls and tangles.*

The Bandana Quilts

DIANE RANGER

Blossom, the Bichon Frise puppy that my husband gave me several years ago for my birthday, has been the light of my life. Blossom comes to work with me every day. Gretchen, my office manager, has a toy poodle named Monique that she brings to work with her. Being together almost every day has enabled the two dogs to become best friends.

Gretchen and I made it a habit to take the two dogs to the groomer every week. The groomer would tie a bandana that portrayed the season or an upcoming holiday around Blossom's neck, and put a bow in Monique's hair. Blossom proudly pranced with her new bandana after her trips to the groomer, but oddly, it seemed to disappear within a short time after returning to the office.

As time passed, Gretchen and I became more curious about the mystery of the missing bandanas. After some sleuthing, we discovered that Monique, a very smart, strong-willed poodle, was jealous that only Blossom got a bandana! We observed Monique tugging at the bandana around Blossom's neck until she finally triumphed and pranced away with the coveted scarf. Blossom, having a laid-back, friendly temperament, did not confront Monique, but instead sulked off to her box.

The groomers were initially insistent that a bandana simply wouldn't do for a poodle, which must wear a bow. But finally they consented to giving a bandana to Monique also. Our problem was solved! Both dogs now pranced proudly, and Monique stopped stealing Blossom's bandana.

One day while cleaning, we found a hidden stash of stolen bandanas in the back of Monique's box. It gave me an idea. My mother and my grandmother have always made their children and grandchildren quilts. I received the last quilt that my grandmother made and I always felt that it made my cousins a little jealous. I quickly gathered my abundant collection of Blossom's bandanas and shipped them off to my mother, playfully reminding her that she had not yet made a quilt for her "granddaughter" Blossom.

When Blossom's finished quilt arrived, Monique was characteristically disappointed. I asked Mama to make a second bandana quilt for Monique. After its arrival, Gretchen and I loved watching the determined little poodle tug it from room to room as her portable bed. This was no easy feat since it was several times her size.

Blossom also loves her quilt and sleeps on it every day. She was truly the greatest gift I have ever received. I thank God for her every single time I look into her face and she responds with an expressive, cute look. I have learned to treasure her as I do my family. When I become lonely for my family, I know how blessed I am to have the quilt from my grandmother. It doesn't take me long to feel connected once again simply by cuddling the treasure my grandmother left me.

■ *A reusable masking tape is available to help quilters keep their hand stitching uniform. It has printed lines to show nine or twelve stitches per inch. Quilters place the tape along the lines to be quilted and follow the lines as they go.*

■ *A rule of thumb for machine stitching is ten stitches per square inch.*

■ *Sometimes machine quilting will leave noticeable needle holes in a cotton fabric quilt. The area can be misted with cool water to close the holes. The moisture makes the cotton fibers relax and fill in the holes left by the stress created by the needle.*

Love for Louisa

JUDITH ALLEN ZINN

Louisa was a tall woman with straight posture who, after the birth of seven children, was a little "round" through the middle. There was a kindness and beauty in her sad brown eyes that everyone loved. In those days, her name was pronounced *Loo-eye-zah*. She was my maternal grandmother.

When I was growing up, my family visited Grandma Louisa and Grandpa Sam during the summers. When I wasn't playing, or swimming, or sailing on Lake Pulaski, Grandma and I spent precious time alone with each other sitting on her big screened porch while she taught me to embroider. I sat in front of her and mirrored her stitching because she was left-handed and I was right-handed.

When I was in grade school, she made a

quilt for me. At that time, I did not appreciate the treasure I had. I loved it because Grandma made it. The quilt was peach color and had white kittens in baskets on it. It was on my bed during my childhood and then became my prized possession as I grew older and began to fully appreciate the art of quilting.

At the end of my senior year of high school, we moved to another town but did not have enough room to take everything with us. My mother packed items in large trunks that were sent to my sister's house and stored in her garage. My quilt was in one of those trunks. I was away at college when I learned that a flood filled my sister's basement and garage. My heart was broken when I learned that my quilt was ruined and cast away.

Years later, I developed a deep and strong love of needlework. Looking back, I think that it is not just because of a love of the art itself but also a love of the precious times spent alone with Grandma. My stitching lessons with her were special time spent together — just the two of us. Now, as an adult, I am a quilter. One Christmas I sat reading through some treasures that "Santa" brought to me. I began to leaf through a reproduction of an early *Quilter's*

Newsletter when, to my joy, I discovered a copy of the very pattern of the quilt that my dear Grandma had made for me. Tears sprang to my eyes. It felt like she was there with me. I reproduced the quilt as a wall hanging in dedication to Grandma. In the middle, I quilted the likeness of my *right* hand crossing over her *left* hand to symbolize the debt of love I owed to her. The hands were inside a quilted, feathered heart to show that she kindly and lovingly taught me.

My Grandmother Louisa Tan Walters gave me a treasure that I will never lose. The love for needlework has been my good companion for these many years. Because of love *expressed* during very special times spent alone with Grandma, I developed a passion for the *expression*. I now teach the art of hand appliqué and hand quilting. Grandma's example created a profound desire within me to keep the art of needlework alive.

■ *If you don't like using a thimble, you can save your fingertips by wearing rubber gloves, placing small pieces of moleskin, black electrical tape, white plumber's tape, masking tape, surgical tape, or paper tape on the tips of fingers that are held under the quilt. An over-the-counter Band-Aid liquid or clear nail polish can also be brushed on the fingertips.*

■ *Soothe sore fingers by washing dishes in hot soapy water, soaking in hydrogen peroxide, coating with lip balm overnight, and applying aloe vera lotion.*

Succeeding Against
the Odds

MARY MAYFIELD

We were experiencing another snowstorm. Several inches of snow had fallen and the roads in southeastern, central, and northern Nebraska were becoming ice-packed. Bitter cold wind blew the snow around, making it hard to see, but since I had been born and raised in Nebraska, that was nothing new.

Even though we were used to having weather like this, I was in a quandary. This was the weekend that the women of the Evangelical Lutheran Church of America were to hold a service weekend. Three times a year, women from across Nebraska met at a designated place and devoted an entire weekend to serving in whatever way they were needed. It didn't matter what the need — from decorating a new building to making and hanging curtains — the ladies came.

Those of us on the planning board wondered if we should cancel this particular weekend because of the weather. But after placing a few phone calls, we discovered that these determined women were committed to completing the task at hand. Many were farm folks who were not accustomed to putting off what needed to be done.

Nearly all the churches in Nebraska have a history of quilting bees. They were the women's social gatherings, their entertainment, a way to be creative, feel useful, and serve the Lord because many of the quilts were given to the needy. That was our assignment for this weekend: quilting blankets and banners.

Our destination was the Campus Lutheran Center at the University of Nebraska in Kearney. For many this was a long drive. The roads could only be navigated at a snail's pace and the tension of doing so in these weather conditions was exhausting. Some gals had to stop for the night at a hotel and continue their quest in the morning. One lady's husband chauffeured her to the destination, stayed in a motel the whole weekend, then chauffeured her home. Cars were in ditches and medians all along the roads. As the time approached, I was surprised when thirteen cold and road-weary women from all around the state of Nebraska assembled to receive instructions for the weekend's project. Only two ladies had cancelled out.

Having seen our work before, the Campus Lutheran Center at the University of Nebraska charged us to "give the place some color and life" by making and hanging seven banners that represented the six seasons of the church year. The church year is color coded and the seasonal colors can be seen in vestments, stoles, and church banners.

As I introduced the project to the ladies and explained that our deadline was that Sunday morning, they were still exhausted from the strain of driving on icy roads, so they felt overwhelmed by the scope and limited time for us to accomplish the goal. They were convinced that there was no way to accomplish this task in the time allotted. Discouraged, they wouldn't even pick up the simple patterns that I had laid on the floor in the middle of the circle where we were sitting.

In desperation, I opened the suitcase I had packed with the beautiful, brightly colored fabric I had selected for the banners. There were twelve to fifteen shades of each of the six church colors. Suddenly the women seemed as if they had taken an energy pill. They came alive, their eyes widened, smiles appeared on their faces, and soon the room was buzzing with excitement as the group planned. Ladies who had never seen each other before became friends and paired up. A mother and daughter formed a team and decided to work together. The conversation became lively.

"I want the blues for the Advent season."

"I'll take the whites for Christmas."

"Pass me the greens for Epiphany."

"I like the purples for Lent."

"Can I do Easter? I love those golds!"

"The reds are fantastic. I'll work on those for the Day of Pentecost."

"Well, that leaves the Sundays after Pentecost. I'll take the second palette of greens for that banner."

Isn't it interesting what colorful fabrics overflowing from an old suitcase will do for the spirit?

The progress was unbelievably strong. Some students from the university helped cut fabric and lay out blocks. One pinned, one sewed, and another ironed. We selected several very simple strip-piecing techniques and the banners quickly took shape throughout the weekend. We hung the last banner just as the processional was getting started on Sunday morning.

Each banner held its own beauty, but when grouped together in the display, the blended hues were incredibly breathtaking. The emotions of the ladies ran high as they gazed at their creations. Their diligent efforts to combat the challenges of weather and time had paid off and the beautiful banners before us would be used year after year.

Like the quilting bees of old, in one short weekend, friendships were forged, love exchanged, new techniques learned, and ideas shared. These banners are works of art to be proud of. A quilt in any form is a treasure — a special gift handcrafted as a reflection of the heart.

CHAPTER 2

Heirloom Memories

*Blessed are
the quilters,
for they are the
piecemakers.*

The Wedding Quilt: A Tradition of Comfort

NAOMI RHODE

Anna Goodman was an Icelandic immigrant who had come to the United States at the age of sixteen and married George, her sweetheart, also from Iceland. They settled on the plains of North Dakota, in a sod house with one room downstairs and a loft up above. The winters were bitter cold, with the snow often blowing high up over the few windows that exposed the world outside.

The summers were built around the hope of a good harvest, but the crops were often plagued by swarms of grasshoppers, scorching heat, prairie rain, or hailstorms. Eking out a living in this strange land was a continuing struggle.

However, Anna was tenacious, creative, strong, and loving. Soon the babies started coming — every two years for twenty-eight years. Three of them died in infancy, the grief further compounding their challenging life.

When their children went to bed in the loft they could hear the spinning wheel whirring late into the night, along with the creaking of the lumber that supported the sod roof and walls. Anna was spinning yarn from the sheep they raised so that she could make clothing for her family of thirteen. Wool socks, mittens, sweaters, baby clothing — all made to insulate her loved ones from the drafty existence inside, and the subzero temperatures outside.

The soft carded wool was also used for the stuffing of quilts made from flour sacks and pieces of fabric that could be gleaned from old garments or bedding.

The one project that took most of Anna's time and love was the wedding quilt. As each child left home to start his or her own family, Anna, or "Amma" as we called her ("Grandma" in Icelandic), would create a masterpiece. She would sacrifice wool that could have been used for stockings or sweaters to fill the wedding quilt. Each couple was told that this was their special wedding gift from both George and Anna.

My mother, Ellen Borg, the first girl to

be born and live to adulthood, was also the first girl to receive her quilt when she left home to marry handsome, dark-haired Virgil Reed. Of course, the quilt was on their bed the first night — and every night of their marriage. It got ragged and needed new covers from time to time, but it was the "wedding blessing" over their bodies — and their marriage — meant to warm and comfort them.

When my father died suddenly at the age of fifty-one, my mother was heartbroken. Their marriage had been a wonderful one, and in losing him, she had lost her very dearest friend. The quilt was quietly taken off the bed, folded up, and placed in a box. She could not bear to sleep under this precious treasure alone.

Years passed and it was time for my wedding to Jim Rhode. Knowing of my mother's meager finances, I wondered what her wedding gift would be. I watched her face as I opened the box that she gave. When I saw what was inside, I was shocked and moved to tears. She had taken her wedding quilt, re-covered the precious wool, and given it to us. Her words were poignant and powerful.

"Naomi, dear, this is no longer 'just a quilt.' It has become a 'comforter.' It has lovingly warmed and comforted your dad and me through our entire married life. It has held our tears, and heard our laughter. It has shared the warmth of our love with you and your brother on those cold mornings when you hopped into bed with us. Even more than that, it has reminded us of "The Comforter," the spirit of God that comes to us, resides within us, and comforts our journey with joy, hope, love, and peace. Sleep well, dear children, as your father and I did. May it always remind you of our love and comfort — and of God's."

It did. Every night we slept under the wedding comforter and knew of its blessings! It warmed us in the winter, and even cooled us in the summer, if that could possibly be true! We were blessed with three children, who snuggled with us and felt warmed under our special quilt through the years.

When we moved into a new home and bought a king-sized bed, our quilt looked dwarfed.

Retaining its blessings in our hearts, I neatly folded the quilt and put it into a box.

A few years later, the first of my three children, who had snuggled in bed with us on Saturday mornings, was getting married. I thought of the tattered quilt and pulled it out of its resting place. The wool was matted and crunched into the corners. It was lumpy in the middle. But I had an idea. This marvelous tradition that had blessed our early years together could not be broken.

I carefully divided the wool from my wedding comforter into three portions. I found a friend's mother, a quilter par excellence, and had her make three wonderful quilts. Augmented with some other filling material, the wool was lovingly placed into three different king-sized quilts. Each had patterns that were intricately designed, color coordinated, and were a long way from the flour sacks of that first wedding quilt from the plains of North Dakota.

As we presented each new couple with their quilt, I told them its story and repeated my mother's words.

Years have passed. Now there is another generation. Twelve wonderful children born to our three children: the great-great-grandchildren of Anna and George, great-grandchildren of Virgil and Ellen, and grandchildren of Jim and Naomi. And they snuggle with their parents under a very special quilt on cold Saturday mornings.

It is no surprise to me that they call me "Amma." When they are married, there will be a symbolic gift given. It will include one-hundred-year-old wool from the sheep of a simple Icelandic farm couple who migrated to the plains of North Dakota. A couple who believed in passing their love, comfort, care, and prayers, in a tangible way, to the next generation. Soon there will be four generations of "comforted" people. As they start their families, unseen angels surround them bringing love, peace, and happiness to these new marriages and the children to come.

"One woman quilts and begins to gather a sense of wholeness from the fragments of her life. Another quilts to help mend the world's brokenness. Still another woman takes up her needle to hand a legacy of warmth and love to her children — a legacy that will continue into the next generation and the next."

— ALICE KALSO,
Life Stories Told in Stitches

■ ■ ■

Summer quilts are not lined with batting, making them lighter for sleeping in hot weather.

Seasons of Time

JUNE STEWARD

World War II was a terrible time in history. Only those who lived through that period can begin to understand its agonies. To be a teenager during those days brought incredible problems, dread, and distress. Many young men enlisted in the armed forces to get into the branch of service they preferred, but all the boys who had reached the age of eighteen were required to be registered for the draft. All were men of courage, bravery, a love of country, and a sense of duty and determination to protect family and freedoms.

Those of us left behind were tormented by our emotions, questioning if we would ever see our loved ones again. We were determined to do whatever we could to help win the war and get our soldiers home again. Time and personal sacrifices were gladly given. Wives and mothers worked in war plants, and for many, this was the first time they had worked outside the home. As teenagers, my friends and I worked in the Red Cross stations rolling bandages, knitting socks for the soldiers, and writing letters. We were extremely lonely. We spent recreational hours working on time-consuming needlework that was placed in our hope chests as we awaited their return. With surging patriotism, tears would roll down our faces as we sang "God Bless America," hoping and waiting to hear that the war was over.

Ward was the boy next door. His mother owned the apartment my family rented, and from the time I moved in, Ward and I were instant friends and did many things together. We played croquet, went swimming, did chores for our parents, rode bicycles, played basketball in the streets, and went to movies together. During the hot days of summer, we would spread a blanket under the fruit trees with glasses of freshly made lemonade, enjoying the breezes while we chatted. He often serenaded me with lighthearted little songs during our times together. At night, he would sometimes throw tiny pebbles at my bedroom window until I acknowledged him, just so he could say good night.

One by one, our friends were being called into active service and because of this, Ward began to feel that his number would soon be called. His lighthearted little ditties that he used to sing became songs sung with an expression of longing and tenderness. He would sing, "Don't sit under the apple tree with anyone else but me . . . 'til I come marching home," and, "I'll be with you in Apple Blossom Time. I'll be with you to change your name to mine. One day in May . . . church bells will chime. You will be mine, in Apple Blossom Time." The lyrics and music became the expressions of our hearts and helped us get through that horrible time of war.

When the papers came in the mail from the draft board, Ward was required to report to the public library and from there he would soon be shipped out. It was a hard time for everyone. The new soldiers and their families knew that this might be the last time they saw each other.

It was no different for Ward, his mother, and me. We went as far as we could go with him, the entrance of the building, but it did not seem nearly enough. We watched through the ominous glass door as we saw Ward take his place in a long line of draftees, stripped to his waist, in his bare feet, getting shots. Then the large group of young men were taken out the back door, put on a bus, and taken away. His mother was so grieved that when we returned to the car, all she could do was lean, for a long period of time, over the steering wheel, crying out to God for his safety. I felt so helpless.

Ward was wounded in action and was sent to a hospital in England, where he recovered and then was discharged on December 6, 1945. He arrived home and still in his uniform he picked me up from my house and took me to the loveliest overlook in our hometown of Cincinnati. It was a cold, crisp winter night and the lights of the city looked especially brilliant. Ward proposed to me that night and we were married in May 1946, in apple blossom time.

One beautiful October day, five months into our married life, my mother-in-law arrived unannounced on the doorstep. We chatted a bit, and then she said, "You need to make a quilt." My own mother never had time to make quilts. She had to work outside the home to help provide food, clothing, and to pay the bills. I had never even made one single quilt block. But quilting was my mother-in-law's passion and hobby. She and I talked about the material we would use and she returned the next day with a pattern that she had cut from cardboard. She showed me how to fold the material to cut several pieces at a time and how to arrange them to form the pattern. She also told me how many of each to cut.

Ward worked evenings so I occupied my time with the quilt when he was gone. The evenings were lonely. Perhaps Mother knew that making a quilt would help me pass the solitary hours, and I am sure she hoped her passion for quilting would become my passion as well.

I worked hard, having always been taught that you finished what you started. Finally, the top was completed. I borrowed a quilting hoop and hand quilted the only way I knew — small stitches that went through the top, batting, and lining. By spring I was two-thirds done and was so tired of working on the quilt that I felt I would never get it finished. My husband gave me a new Singer sewing machine and when I found out it had a new quilting attachment, I was inspired to finish my quilt the easy way. So I used the new quilting attachment, but the machine puckered the fabric in places, and the work looked terrible alongside the fine hand stitches. I felt I had ruined it, but at last the red-and-white quilt was finished!

After we had been married for about two years, we moved to a new home. Again my dear mother-in-law came, this time carrying a big bundle. She presented us with a very large appliquéd quilt of her own design for our bed. To her it was another project — a quilt, of which she was proud, made for our new home with much love, warmth, and blessing. Imagine my surprise when I unwrapped it. The quilt burst with apple blossoms! Did she know about the songs her son used to sing to me while we courted? I don't know.

We have been married for nearly fifty-five years. In reflection, I have thought about how the seasons of an apple tree can be compared to our marriage. An apple tree has beauty as well as hardships in every season. In the springtime, the blossoms of the apple tree exude a fragrance that invites one to spread a blanket and linger.

In the summertime, its shade offers comfort. In autumn, its branches bend low with luscious, nourishing fruit, that also announces that it's time to get busy and preserve the fruit so that you might enjoy healthy, delicious nutrition all through the winter.

In wintertime, its gnarled, twisted, and broken branches, some propped and braced, form a stark silhouette against the bitter winter sky. And winter's most exhilarating and beautiful treasure — the newly fallen snow — bears down the branches, glistening and enhancing, showing the charm of the old apple tree.

Similarly, in the springtime of our lives, Ward and I suffered many killing frosts of insecurities and anguishes, but we survived, and experienced the awesome beauty of budding young life. We could never have realized the palette we spread for ourselves under the apple tree long ago would yield fragrances that have lingered for all these years.

In the summertime of our lives, there was the shelter, protection, and comfort of our own home as our children were born and raised. There has been no joy like that of observing them grow into what they are today, each evidencing qualities and gifts we could not have imagined. Their lives have brought such refreshment and fulfillment to us.

In the autumn of our lives, the children

began to leave us and establish homes of their own. We recognized these "new trees" now were beginning to show fruitfulness. We have gratefully observed them as they cultivate, shield, protect, and constantly nourish the family values now being reproduced "after its kind."

Now in the wintertime of our lives, when we are feeling somewhat like the gnarled silhouettes of the apple trees, we realize we are being renewed daily by the great hand of God and may have many years yet to yield fruitful influence on our family and friends. Each season has its hard times, beauties, and rewards, but the benefits of wintertime are many and bring revitalization to all of God's creations. I find myself basking in the fragrances of the memories stitched together by time.

■ *A shorter, thinner needle is easier to maneuver in and out of the quilt, giving the quilter better control and enabling her to create smaller stitches.*

■ *When working on a large quilt project, needles should be changed often. Extended use may cause needles to dull, bend, or break.*

■ *Try to keep hands as dry as possible when working on a quilt project. The moisture from your hands may oxidize the needle, turning it black. The needle will then stick when trying to create small stitches.*

■ *Cut thread lengths eighteen inches or no longer than an arm's length. Sew with a single length of thread. Knot the longer end to be cut off later.*

My Inheritance

LIBBY KACZYNSKI

My mother, Mary, was a perfectionist. The wife of an Italian builder living in Cleveland, Ohio, during the early part of the twentieth century, Mom was the keeper of their household and had a strong work ethic. She was an expert at cooking, cleaning, and sewing. As a child, I felt that she had many talents that didn't seem to have been passed down to me. Try as I might to live up to her expectations, I always felt imperfect.

After her four children grew up, married, and moved out, Mother took up the art of quilting. She created her own patterns, of course, and made quilts for each of her four children and their spouses. I was in awe; my admiration and appreciation of her talents grew with each quilt she completed. Then, as her fifteen grandchildren came along, she created a special quilt for each of them. What a wonderful legacy she was building! No two were alike. The color combinations and patterns seemed to reflect something special about the person for whom it was created. I remember seeing the looks of happiness and appreciation on the faces of the recipients when the quilt was presented to them. Feeling that I did not possess any of my mother's creative abilities, I could only dream about passing along something of similar value to my family someday.

My husband, Len, and I, along with my three siblings and our families, all lived within an hour's drive of each other in the Cleveland metropolitan area. We were all fortunate to live within a short distance of Mother and Father. Family gatherings were exciting events. The food was delicious, the conversation lively, and the rambunctious activities of the grandchildren playing always resulted in one or more of them getting into trouble.

Many of the gatherings involved the women of the family viewing and marveling about the colors or patterns of a newly started quilt or the beauty of a newly finished creation. The quilt-making process seemed like a daunting task to me, but Mother seemed to thrive with the challenge. As she got older, the process took progressively longer to complete, but the end result was no less beautiful. After sixty-six years of marriage, my father, Tony, passed away in 1979. Mother died in 1985.

When my husband, Len, retired, we purchased a house in Florida. After we settled in, we found that there was a quilt shop nearby. One day I decided to check it out. I fell in love! Going into the shop gave me the same feeling as many others experience when going into a chocolate factory or ice cream shop. The colors, the fabrics, the patterns, everything! I was hooked. I became a student of the art, buying books, borrowing from libraries, taking lessons, and joining quilt clubs to learn.

I watched every quilting program on television that I could, went to every quilt show I heard about within driving distance, and practiced, practiced, practiced. As I started to successfully make quilts of my own, a sense of intense pride welled up inside me. I could almost see my mother smiling and approving. Perhaps I *had* inherited some of her talents after all. I felt sad that my mother didn't live long enough to see any of *my* quilts. Perhaps then she could have seen that some of her talent lived on in me. My sister paints, my brother carves wood, but *I* can quilt. As my skills grew, I began to make quilts for my four children and their spouses, and then my seven grandchildren.

Taking a lesson from the tradition started by my mother, each member of my family has her own personalized quilt, in a color combination and pattern specifically chosen for her, sewn with my love.

Now I am sewing quilts for my three great-grandchildren. For this new generation, I have established a new quilting tradition. I have a photo of Len and me that I have transferred to fabric and sew onto the back of each quilt that I make. So not only does the recipient get my signature on her special quilt, she gets a picture to connect her memories with us. I have my mother to thank for my inspiration, my love for family tradition, and for my hidden talent. I may never be the perfectionist that Mother was, but what I did inherit from her was the ability to pass on a legacy of love to my family members, wrapped up in the fabric of their own quilts.

■ *Orally transmitted stories passed on through the years have told of quilts being used during the nineteenth century to carry hidden messages for runaway slaves using the Underground Railroad to escape.*

No one suspected a quilt hung over a tree branch or fence, with the pretense of being aired out to dry, could be a way of guiding the runaway slaves on a safe route while traveling on their way to freedom.

A code was worked into the quilt patterns that would warn Underground Railroad travelers of danger, communicate directions, or let them know if they were near a home that would be safe for them to take refuge.

Because the slaves were not allowed to learn to read or write, words were never used or written down using this form of communication. The coding was passed on by word of mouth, sometimes connecting symbols from African culture and history to familiar quilt patterns, to relay the necessary messages.

The Quilt That Never Was

RALPH HOOD

One of my most prized possessions is a piece of a quilt — not the entire quilt, mind you, but only a piece. In fact, the entire quilt never really existed, and thereby, as Shakespeare said, hangs a tale.

My great-grandmother, Eliza Boulware Stokes, was married in South Carolina in 1851. Thirteen of her Salem College classmates set out to make a friendship quilt for Eliza's wedding gift. Each young lady carefully stitched one square of the quilt. Twelve squares were of equal size; the single center square was four times the size of the smaller squares. The completed squares were to be sewn together to make up the complete friendship quilt. The center square now hangs on the wall of my home, complete with a penned-on note

104

dating from about 1910 handwritten by Annie, who was Eliza's daughter and my grandmother's sister. That note briefly outlines as follows the story of the quilt that never was:

Before Eliza's wedding, one of the thirteen friends died, and the squares were never joined together. We must assume that the death so disrupted the lives of the remaining young ladies that they just never got around to completing the quilt. Eliza did get the individual squares, however, and kept them carefully, no doubt planning to complete the quilt someday.

Future plans often go unfulfilled, and the Civil War dominated Eliza's life during the 1860s and for many years thereafter.

Eliza and her husband lived on a farm in Colleton County, South Carolina. During the war, her husband fought with the Confederate army, and Eliza, like other southern women of the era, coped as best she could. Toward the end of the war, Eliza got word that Sherman's army — on the now-famous march to the sea — would pass directly through Colleton County. So the enemy would not confiscate it and use it to further their cause, Eliza wrapped the family silverware in the quilt squares, packed the silver-filled squares in trunks, and buried the trunks on the bank of the Edisto River. She then departed with her family to Winnsboro, South Carolina, to escape the coming conflict.

Oddly, Sherman did not come through Colleton County, but did go right through Winnsboro, where Eliza stood on the front porch of her borrowed cabin and refused to allow the Union soldiers entry.

Upon Eliza's return, the trunks were dug up and remained unopened for quite some time, as Eliza and her family struggled with the problems of life in the war-ravaged South. When Eliza finally opened the trunks, she found the silverware in perfect shape, and the quilt squares marred only by small brown water stains. Those stains are clearly visible on the square that hangs in my home today.

The other squares are widely scattered among the descendants of Eliza Boulware Stokes. No one person has more than one square. Had the quilt been completed, it would have been used, worn out, and discarded during those tough years of long ago. Instead, the efforts of thirteen friends — more than a century and a half ago — live on in thirteen different homes, telling a story of friendship, family, and American history.

During the Civil War a "quilting bee" was called a "quilting frolic," "quilting party," or simply "quilting."

■ ■ ■

Readers of twentieth-century women's magazines would send their quilt designs to be published. Commercial pattern companies would make up names for the designs inspired by the times. Civil War memories produced pattern names like "Union Star" that reflected the winning side.

Americana

CAROLINA FERNANDEZ

Leslie and I have been the closest of friends since the fifth grade, when we were serendipitously placed together in Mr. Hunter's homeroom. We remained best friends all through high school, sharing cheerleading chants, prom nights, field trip bus rides, and a trip to Europe as teenagers. My mother always called us "two peas in a pod." We settled on different colleges and grad schools, but nonetheless remained bonded — she was a bridesmaid at my wedding, I sang at hers. Afterward, Leslie ultimately settled in Philadelphia while I wound up in Kentucky, but even so, we made frequent visits to each other's homes, forged relationships with each other's mates, and loved each other's kids as if they were our own.

After living apart for twenty-five years,

fate brought us together when my husband accepted a promotion to New York, and we bought a house in Connecticut. Leslie and I were now a mere three and a half hours away by car. She came to see our new place on its rolling, wooded lot. Before dinner, the children were boating around our pond and we were washing the romaine while chatting counterside. She commented that many of her friends on the "Mainline" had homes far more physically impressive than ours, but that ours would always be a "memory house" for her kids.

Her comment brought back the memory of her childhood home and how much of a "memory house" it was for me. I shared with her what I remembered.

Set on twenty-one acres of lush Pennsylvania soil, skirted by a white split-rail fence, and reached by a long curving driveway, her home was where we played hide-and-seek around the koi-stocked fishpond. It was where we always ate more dough than cookies from the slice-and-bake chocolate chip roll; where we tobogganed down their massive hill; and where we spent sleep overs on the back widow's walk under the stars.

Of course, as a kid I never appreciated her parents' collection of American antiques, original oils, and accessories reflecting the decorative arts that I am now passionate about, especially the heirloom quilts dressing the guest room beds.

Later, when we wound up in our shared hometown on the weekend of our twenty-fifth high school reunion, Leslie wanted me and the kids to come over to her parents' house. She wanted to play together by reminiscing about our golden childhood and then rummage through previously unnoticed pieces of Americana.

Antiques, art, almost anything hand-crafted, are in my blood, and as any collector will quickly admit, once they get in your blood they are practically impossible to get out. So I did what any lover of things beautiful would do: I stood intrigued by all of the artwork, ran my fingers down the hand-rubbed, cherry, tall case clock, read carefully the wording on the hand-painted frakturs, and examined the spindles on the antique Windsors.

When we got to the guest room and her mother lovingly unfolded the quilt on the double bed, it was with a gentleness that could hardly go unnoticed. She talked fondly of how her grandmother had hand stitched each square of fabric and then pieced them together with perfect symmetry, how she had hand stitched the lining to the coverlet in the most beautiful pattern, and how evenly her stitches were spaced. She talked of the perfectionism that went into every stitch, the love, and the many hours that went into the quilt.

Then she walked over to the antique blanket chest and opened it as one might open an heirloom antique Bible — slowly, gingerly. It revealed a half-dozen more quilts, all neatly folded between tissue paper, every one as beautifully handmade as the one on the bed. We guessed the names of the patterns with some futility, but with each examination, we admitted that one was just as beautiful as the next. Each quilt must have its own story, we reflected, lost with the death of its maker, but nonetheless the quilts before us have been admired for three successive generations.

That's the way it goes with quilts, as with all things handmade. Each has a maker. Each maker started with inspiration. Who knows from where the inspiration came for these quilted treasures?

Who knows the conditions that led a woman to pause in her day to stitch? Was it when babies cried in the background, or when they napped; when older children needed help with writing, or when they played outside? Could it have been when dinner needed to be prepared, or when it was in the oven; when laundry beckoned its relentless call, or when it was drying; at night by the glow of candlelight with children bedded down, or in broad daylight when they were out playing hopscotch? Did she stitch when she was sad and lonely, or when she was euphoric? Was it when she was contemplative or when she was cross at a rebellious child? Did she stitch to supply a need, as when her children simply needed warm coverings for their cold beds in winter, or did she stitch to provide things of beauty for her home?

Did she ever contemplate with each of those tiny stitches that she was making a thing that might possibly last for two hundred or three hundred years? Did she ever reflect on the fact that her great-grandchildren might fight over who got to keep this family heirloom? Did she ever let herself glow in the vision of what that great-grandchild might look like? If the child would have her nose or Grandpa's eyes? Or did she wonder who they might marry? Did she ever stop to think if any one of her offspring would inherit her love of all things handcrafted, of all things beautiful?

If Leslie and I had been born into a different time and place in history, would we have forged our friendship around a quilting bee rather than under the stars? I am so grateful that some of the women before us opted to use some of their time in the calm and gentle, womanly pursuit of working stitches with their tired hands. Certainly, we are all the better for it.

■ *Store finished quilts in pie safes, blanket chests, cedar chests, dressers, large covered baskets, bookcases, armoires, and linen closets as well as on clothes rack, open shelves, and quilt racks.*

■ *Store quilts in a spot that is away from light, moderate in temperature, well ventilated, dry, and clean.*

■ *Do not use plastic bags to store quilts — they can trap moisture and pests, causing mildew and other damage.*

■ *Place quilts that are on display in a dryer every two or three weeks on low heat to remove dust.*

Under the Quilt Frame

ELAINE MEYLAN

We were raised under the quilt frame with a view of sturdy black shoes and silk stockings rolled just below the knees. Above us, there was an expanse of white cotton backing. The smells of strong coffee and cinnamon rolls mixed with the aroma of old ladies' feet. The poke and pull of six skillful needles followed the light blue highways mapped out upon the quilt. All the while, we heard the constant chatter of ladies who were friends, farm wives, citizens of the country, citizens of the community, mothers, daughters, and sisters above us.

We were sisters, often staying at Grandma's and privy to the weekly meeting of the Ladies' Aid Society where quilts were quilted to raise money for missions. "Grandma, what are missions?" one sister asked from under the frame. She didn't have to emerge from her cozy spot under the frame where paper doll families were neatly arranged because her grandma not only heard the grown-up conversations *above* the quilt frame but also the small voices *underneath*.

"Missions money goes to support missionaries, who work in far-off places telling people about God," she answered. At that, my sister rearranged her paper dolls to form a family that was preparing to go on a long missionary journey.

Overhead, the chatter continued as fashion was discussed. Political problems from the national and local news were solved. We learned who should and who should not run for office and why. We heard the "pet peeves" that wives had regarding their husbands, but we also heard praise for the men who worked hard, sacrificed much, and provided for their families.

As we grew, we no longer felt comfortable under the quilt frame. We eventually went away to college and left the rural community of our grandmother.

Today my sisters and I measure our wealth by the quilts we have made and are planning to make out of the colorful fabric waiting in boxes on shelves. We feel that there is no greater honor than to be invited to see someone's quilts or, when we have guests, to invite them on a quilt tour of our home. As the history of each quilt is shared, the guest is linked to our family, to the saga, and to our souls.

The skillful needles still poke and pull through the thickness of fabric. Tiny white stitches still follow the blue highways mapped out upon the quilt. The layers of fabric are experiences and memories being quilted together to form our lives. The blue highways are the decisions we have made. The quilters mapped them years ago. The Ladies' Aid Society still meets, but on celestial ground. My sisters and I are still under the quilt frame.

"Just as the pieces of the quilt are sewn together with interlocking stitches, all people are linked together in the fabric of our world. In a way, the patchwork quilt represents all the different people of the world. We are individual in our attitudes, lifestyles, and backgrounds, yet we share so much of what it means to be human."

— TERESA GUSTAFSON,
Love Is a Blanket

■ ■ ■

Mount Pelée, Martinique, 1902

Mary Louise Smith

Quilting has evolved into a unique art form. Quilts were made for practical uses such as bed blankets and wraps, but these same quilts have become valuable, depicting special events, showing our heritage and family folklore. Today quilting is more popular than ever. With the invention of the sewing machine and new technical tools, quilting has expanded to include all expressions of the quilter's imagination and creativity.

"Mount Pelée, Martinique, 1902" is such a quilt. It embodies my heritage by capturing the beauty and richness of my paternal grandfather's homeland, and as a visual legacy to my children. It also holds a special memory of my beloved grandfather. I remember the stories he told, especially one of the great eruption of Mount Pelée in 1902. While some people around the world slept comfortably in their beds, Mount Pelée erupted, stretching her fiery arms, embracing everything in her path, including thirty-five thousand of the inhabitants of the town of St. Pierre.

As a small child, my grandfather fled the eruption in a crowded fishing boat, cradled in his mother's arms. The people in that small boat rowed until just offshore, to escape the rumbling of the volcano. Everyone on the boat was frightened, wailing, and pointing to the island. What my grandfather saw was a wondrous sight. He saw a sky that was alive with bright, fiery lava that looked like "shooting stars." In his eyes, it was beautiful as the "shooting stars" cascaded toward the sea, fizzled out, and disappeared.

My grandfather and his mother were the only two in our bloodline who escaped. Sadly, the rest of my paternal family was among those who did not make it to the safety of the sea.

When my grandfather told the story of Mount Pelée, I remember trying to envision the fiery "shooting stars." How I wished that I, too, had been there to see this wondrous sight. The tragedy of the event had escaped my grandfather in his innocence. The impact of the loss of family did not register until later years. "Beauty is in the eyes of the beholder" comes to mind when I remember my grandfather's story and how he felt that day.

In the seventies, upon visiting my grandfather's homestead in St. Pierre, I saw that the scars of the 1902 eruption were still visible throughout the landscape. I saw Mount Pelée, rising 4,428 feet up, head hidden in the clouds, a serene, majestic giant. She stood regally, like a queen surveying her domain below, an awesomely beautiful sight to behold. That day she earned my greatest respect and admiration. Pelée means "fire goddess." Mount Pelée was indeed the fire goddess — one to be admired, yet one to be feared for her all-consuming power.

The experience I had was so powerful that I decided to record the memories in fabric by making a quilt. As an American of both French European and Caribbean descent, I felt this quilt would be a way to record a piece of history and connect my son and daughter to a people, a homeland, and a culture on a distant island in the Caribbean called Martinique. "Mount Pelée, Martinique, 1902" was not made for the bed. It measures sixty-nine by forty-six inches. It is a cherished quilt, created especially as a legacy of my paternal ancestral homeland. The quilt is my original design and has six eighteen-inch blocks, four of which are abstract silhouettes of people, flora, fauna, and homes. The fifth block is the French fleur-de-lis, as Martinique is a French commonwealth. The sixth is the Hawaiian lei, for remembrance and renewal of life. The fabric colors I chose for the silhouettes are the same as those used in the national, brightly colored, plaid madras costumes of the island women. I chose the colors black and brown to symbolize the lives lost. The background of each block has an echo stitch, which surrounds the image in a ripple effect, to give the quilt a sense of motion alluding to the molten lava flow. Orange fabric represents the lava surrounding the silhouettes. The quilt is hand-appliquéd and hand-quilted and its black border is machine pieced.

Unlike other immigrants who migrated in vast numbers, only about two dozen Martinican families came to America. Their descendants are few. Unless cultivated in our children, the Martinican culture could disappear when the last Martinican immigrant passes away. Sadly, this could happen in my generation. This quilt is now proudly displayed in my daughter's home, where she tells visitors the story behind the quilt, thereby keeping our history alive.

A quilter's sewing basket should contain:

Scissors for cutting only fabric
Scissors for cutting paper and
*   other materials*
Curved embroidery scissors
Sewing needles
Size 11 machine needles
Needle threader
Thimble
Seam ripper
Measuring tape or ruler
Marking pencils and tailor's chalk
Straight quilter's pins and pincushion
Large safety pins
Glue stick

The Pioneer Spirit

MIKE HARTNETT

The inexhaustible spirit of the pioneer woman is an inspiration to me.

Wives and mothers settled with their families on the harsh plains and mountains of the American West. The land was free in most cases, but it did not come without a price. Although these women came from a variety of backgrounds, they had one thing in common: hardships. We often think about the bad weather with which they had to contend as they tried to cultivate the land. We know that they were in constant threat of Indian attacks. But perhaps one of the most difficult hardships they had to bear was the prevalence of pestilence and disease.

One hardship that we tend to overlook is isolation. Picture a pioneer's little cabin, several hundred miles away from any semblance of civilization and the nearest neighbor often many miles away. The emotional support of a friend was not easily found. These pioneer women provided emotional sustenance to their families but had no one to whom they could turn. Their exhausted husbands could not, in many cases, meet their emotional needs.

Perhaps this is why they eagerly turned to quilting. Very few crafts provide both utilitarian and aesthetic functions like quilting does. One very old pioneer woman was interviewed and asked to describe her feelings about quilting. "I quilted as fast as I could to keep my family warm," she said, "and as beautifully as I could to keep my heart from breaking."

Her words have stayed with me, and I try to remember them whenever I become upset because a grocery store is out of my favorite flavor of ice cream or when facing some other "hardship" of modern life.

Place two mirrors at a ninety-degree angle on two sides of a sample quilt block to see how they would look set together.

■ ■ ■

Many quilts are assembled in an assembly-line fashion. Cut out all of the pieces at once. Follow by stitching the pieces together, then stitching the blocks, then stitching the blocks into the top.

Remembering the Lessons

ROBBY ROBINSON

The best teacher I ever had was my grandmother. She was a lady of the land and its secrets gave her wisdom. She taught me, a young child in Tennessee, to respect and enjoy the land, to be the land's caretaker, and to look to the land for all of my needs.

When she wasn't tending a garden, she was stitching garden motifs into her quilts. "Nature's gardens nourish the body, but a quilted garden warms the body and gives peace to the soul," she would say as she tucked me into bed at night.

She died when I was eleven years old, but I lived with the wealth of her teachings. When I left home to serve my country in Vietnam, my grandmother's words sustained me through the bad days.

Shortly after my arrival, I was assigned to

fly to Da Nang, and while in the helicopter, not knowing what awaited me, I looked down at the countryside. I recognized rice paddies, and forests, but many plots of land were unrecognizable. While gazing, I thought of my grandmother, because the different colors and textures looked like a patchwork garden quilt. That "land garden quilt" gave me comfort, just as my grandmother's fabric garden quilts always did, and suddenly I knew all was well.

Today I have one of "Ma's" garden quilts in my home. It continues to warm my body and bring peace to my soul long after the death of my grandmother. It is almost like having her with me — and it reminds me of the things she taught me.

An important final step in quilt making is the quilter's signature. It can be done on the front or back, in embroidery or with a permanent fabric marker. This provides the recipient with some knowledge of its creative history, and can include a date and other pertinent information.

Works of the Heart

DEBORAH ROSE SAPP

The chain of quilting has looped through our family. As sisters, Ronda and I remember our paternal grandmother, Rosa Mae Sapp, as she sat at a quilting frame that hung from her living room ceiling. We used to love playing under the quilt, pretending it was a tent or a cave. When we got too rambunctious, we would feel the gentle nudge of her foot and hear her say, "You children quiet down." When we crawled out from our pretend shelter, there was always a glint in Grandma's beautiful blue eyes and a smile trying to break across her face.

Many times, while spending the night with Grandma and Grandpa, we were bundled off to bed under several of Grandma's quilts. One time, I complimented Grandma on her sewing skills only to be told, "You could hang a toe in my stitches!" Not quite sure what she meant, I decided it didn't matter; I always felt her love was there to keep us warm.

Our maternal grandmother also quilted, but unfortunately she died before we had a chance to know her. From stories we've been told by our mother, Pearlie Wampler Sapp, Grandma Artie Ellen Wampler was a woman to be much admired. As a small child, she lost most of her right hand in a wood-chopping incident with her older brother. She was left with only her thumb and part of her index finger. This did not deter her from sewing!

She made quilts, but also sewed clothes for her three children, tatted lace, and worked in a hosiery mill for several years. There's not much left of this amazing woman's work, but our mama did receive a piece of one of her quilts from her sister, our Aunt Dorothy Blye. It hangs in an honored place on an upstairs wall in her home. To see such tiny, even stitches and to know that this woman, with patience and love for her family, overcame an obstacle that would cripple most others, makes us all proud of the determination of the women in our family.

The next link in this chain of quilters,

our mother, was not as motivated as her predecessors, but she helped piece several quilt tops. My sister, Ronda, helped Mom piece her first quilt top and then took it to Aunt Dorothy to finish the quilting. Mama has since passed away but her quilt remains as a treasured link in the chain that continues to loop its way through our family.

Ronda has inherited Grandma Wampler's small, even stitching, while I inherited Grandma Sapp's "You can hang a toe in those stitches" style, but we will continue the quilting chain. I hope that someday, someone will look at our quilts and realize that it takes more than material and thread to make a quilt. It takes love, patience, and in some cases, courage to keep families warm and feeling loved under what we call "works of the heart."

CHAPTER 3

Gift Giving

*Good friends are
like quilts —
they never lose
their warmth.*

Patches of Love
The National Donor
Family Council Quilt

MAGGIE COOLICAN

Katie was six, full of personality and spirit. She was an energetic tomboy and her greatest aspiration was to be a mud wrestler when she grew up!

I still remember that bright, beautiful fall morning she walked to the end of our driveway and boarded the school bus all by herself. She was nervous, but I encouraged her independence, saying, "You can do it! I'll be right here watching!" My curly-haired, freckle-faced tomboy bravely skipped down the driveway to the bus. Before boarding, she turned to me with a big dimpled smile. You could tell that she was proud of herself. She waved a big good-bye and was off to school.

About three that day, I received a call from the school. Katie had fallen down on the playground while playing. I arrived at her school in minutes. Never could I have been prepared for what I was to see. Katie was vomiting, twitching, and urinating on the ground. Her left pupil was already dilated, and being a registered nurse, I knew that was a sign of severe brain trauma. In disbelief, I wondered what was happening to my healthy, freckle-faced little girl. It did not appear that Katie even knew that I was there. She was taken to the hospital and was in surgery within the hour.

While we waited in the family room during the nine-hour surgery, the health-care workers, chaplains, and nurses continually supported us. They kept us informed, made telephone calls for us, brought coffee, cried with us, and prayed with us.

Katie survived the surgery and, although in a coma, seemed to respond to pain, which was a good sign. We read to her, talked to her, and played sweet tapes from her first grade classmates. We watched and waited and then waited and watched. The pressure within her head steadily rose and after several days had passed, we watched her deteriorate to a point where we knew we were losing our baby girl.

We kept thinking, "This can't be happening! Children don't die — at least not our child! She is supposed to outlive us!" The week went on and Katie's physicians tried everything possible to save her, but our hopes faded. We noticed that the staff seemed to find it hard to talk to us. They even avoided looking at us now.

My husband and I were strong supporters of the organ donation program and had already made a decision to donate our organs should either of us die, but as for our children? We never even thought about what would happen if our children were to die. There is an assumption that children live to adulthood and make their own decisions. The physicians continued to be evasive as we desperately tried to find some way to make sense out of this seemingly senseless tragedy. We needed to talk this decision over with our other children. They knew that they were losing their sister, but they also felt that they were losing their mom and dad, who were overwhelmed by Katie's terrible trauma. If only we had discussed these things before crisis hit! We now had to make this decision with the added emotion of imminent death.

By the end of the week, Katie was clinically brain dead. Because of the drugs in her body, we were forced to wait two more days, until the drugs used in her treatment were completely out of her system, for an official declaration. During those two days, Katie did not seem dead. She was still breathing. Her heart was still pumping, still warm. Finally, we were permitted to speak to the transplant coordinator, who was sensitive and supportive.

Leaving her that last time, supported by machines but still looking just like our own sleeping Katie, was the most wrenching experience of our lives. During her life, Katie brought many things into our lives such as a special kind of love, a radiance and beauty on a bright spring day, the freedom of a butterfly, and the joy in a child's giggle. It would take time before we could find a purpose in her death, time to accept it, and time to understand that the act of donating would actually make our grieving process easier. We came to understand that her death brought another kind of love, beauty, and joy to four unknown families. Katie's gift of life to these four families allowed us to think of her as still being alive.

After several months passed, I wrote a letter to the hospital explaining how much harder this time was for us because the medical personnel in attendance emotionally withdrew and avoided the whole issue of donation. Because of this letter I was asked to share my experience to help educate the medical personnel to the needs of grieving loved ones. This invitation led to more involvement in speaking to medical personnel to help them understand.

One day I was working on a baby quilt for a friend while traveling in the car. I was a regular quilter. During the children's school years, there was always a teacher having a baby. I found myself cutting out twelve-inch squares to take to the school while this teacher or that teacher was on maternity leave. A block was given to each child in the class so he or she could draw a picture. When completed, I took the squares home and put the blocks together in a "story" quilt for the teacher. While working on a particular quilt, it suddenly hit me — there was comfort and release provided through the making of a quilt! I turned to my husband and said, "Gee, we should make a quilt to help donor families! Families that have shared our experience could send in a square that celebrates the life of their loved one!" My husband thought it was the craziest idea I had ever had.

But that didn't stop me! Modeled after

the quilts I had made for my children's teachers, celebrating a new life being brought into the world, the blocks in this quilt were to be about life — the life of the donor and the new life given because of the donor. I wanted families to remember the loved one they lost in spite of society pressuring us to forget them and move on with our lives. We posted an invitation in a donor family newsletter and immediately started receiving squares for our project. We affectionately called the blocks we received "Patches of Love."

As the "Patches of Love" began to flow in through the mail, we were amazed and blessed by the trust these families placed in us. One block was made out of a wedding dress, another from someone's shirt, a third was crafted from a baby blanket. A picture drawn by a child, a photograph, a patch from a policeman's uniform, someone's locket, and a fisherman's vest are treasures shared through these quilt blocks. Many included a note explaining the meaning behind the portrayal on the block. I was overwhelmed emotionally as I sewed together these patches, filled with so much love. I felt as if I knew every person represented. So many were sent, in fact, that I decided not to make just one quilt, but several hanging panels. The quilt will never be finished. I sew the blocks that I receive into panels, then they are publicly displayed at different events. A special "time for reflection" is set aside for donor families before and after each event. A box, filled with paper, is placed near the quilt for people to record their feelings upon seeing it. A volunteer is always present to provide information and to answer questions.

We had *no* idea the impact that this project would have! In a ripple effect, this visual remembrance, meant to bring comfort to loved ones, captured the attention of others, making them aware of the benefits of donation. This experience has shown me the power that a piece of fabric holds. It can hold a lasting memorial of a loved one. It can hold hope and healing in the midst of loss. It can hold an element that reaches a heart, as nothing else can.

Give the Gift of Life

Maggie Coolican and her family made sense of Katie's death by giving the gift of life to others after the death of their own child. They donated Katie's organs so that others might live.

Please make a decision about organ donation before a crisis hits your family. As Maggie suggests, "If we would consider accepting a donation when a loved one is found to be in need, we should consider becoming a donor."

To learn more about donation, please access the National Kidney Foundation's Web site at www.kidney.org.

You can see actual quilt panels at the National Donor Family Council Web site at www.donorfamilies.org. Touching accounts written in celebration of the generous donor's life can be accessed by clicking on individual "Patches of Love."

■ ■ ■

Wrapped in Hands of Love

DONA ABBOTT

Growing up we had been a very close family. In later years as some of the five children — four girls and a boy — married and moved to other states far away, we were no longer close physically, but we remained emotionally linked. Dad, in particular, missed his brood and tried whenever possible to gather us all together as a family. The Christmas of 1973 was such a time. In preparation for it, I made handcrafted gifts for each member of my family: floor-length quilted skirts for Mom, my three sisters, and my sister-in-law using the colors I knew each person liked, and a tie for my brother.

For Dad, I planned something very special. I wrote to family members asking that they draw an outline of their hands on a favorite piece of old clothing and sign their names. I cut out each hand shape, appliquéd it onto a solid-color sheet, and then embroidered each person's signature and birth date underneath. Our large family — Mom, five children, four grand-children, and three sons- and daughters-in-law — made a generous-sized quilt.

As was our tradition, we all gathered on Christmas Eve to open our gifts, taking turns and enjoying the excitement as each gift was opened and shared. I handed Dad the beautifully wrapped gift box containing the quilt, while everyone in the room waited and watched. Dad opened the box and removed the folded quilt. We could all feel the energy level building since each person present had a small part in helping this quilt become a reality. Dad quickly shook it out to its full size. When he real-ized that the quilt incorporated the hands of each member of his family, his face reg-istered total delight. Wrapping himself up in this new treasure, he rocked from side to side joyfully, saying, "I can never get cold as long as I have my family around me."

As Dad aged, it was his quilt of choice when he snuggled up in his recliner to read or watch television on winter evenings. Over the years the family expanded to in-clude four more grandchildren and eventually several great-grandchildren. To accompany Dad's treasured "hand quilt," Mom made two "hand pillows" incorporating the handprints of the new additions.

The quilt sheltered him through several bouts of cancer, wrapping him with warmth and love at times when I was unable to be with him. He's gone now, but the excitement of seeing the pleasure in his face as he covered himself with that simple homemade quilt warms me to this day.

A lovingly made, hand-sewn quilt warms both the body and the spirit. Some have been painstakingly planned and created, while others have been hastily and haphazardly put together. But no matter how they were constructed, even the crudest represents hours of labor and care.

■ *The best way to store a quilt is to lay it flat, avoiding direct sunlight. Following an Amish method, extra quilts can be stacked and rotated on an unused bed. If this is not possible,* roll them and store them without bending the roll in the middle.

■ *The least desired method for storing a quilt involves folding it. If you do store your quilts in this manner, round the folded edges by stuffing them with acid-free tissue paper or fold it around a cardboard tube. Refold the quilts along new lines periodically.*

■ *Never store a quilt in or under plastic bags. If using cedar or mothballs to discourage pests, be sure that they do not come in contact with the quilt fabric.*

■ *Patchwork and appliqué quilts can be stored creatively and safely in an old pie safe. The punched-tin panels provide ventilation. Use layers of acid-free tissue paper to line the shelves and protect the quilts from the acidity of the wood.*

Grandma's Memory Quilt

PATT BELL

My mother had been caring for my grand-mother at home for several years. However, when Grandmother's throat muscles weak-ened she began having difficulty swallowing her food. Not being able to eat properly made her very weak and unable to walk or transfer herself to a wheelchair. As a family, we decided to move her to a nursing home. It was an emotional time for all of us, but most of all for her. Entering a nursing home was one thing that she had hoped would never happen to her.

By the time she was admitted to the nursing home, her weakened throat mus-cles made her unable to talk. The staff had no connection with her life outside the nursing home, and when bathing her, changing her bedding, or feeding her, it was difficult for them to find a topic of conversation that she could relate to. Dedicated as they were to her care, the staff found themselves taking care of her immediate physical needs without talking to her on a personal level. The family also found it awkward to visit, having to carry on a one-sided conversation.

She celebrated her ninety-fifth birthday shortly after entering the home. For her birthday gift, I purchased a premade quilt. In the center of the back of the quilt, which was white, I stenciled her name, in large letters. Then I stenciled "Mom, Grandma, Great Grandma, Great-Great-Grandma" all around the edge in colors that matched the colors on the front of the quilt. I used coordinating fabric markers to draw stick figures of my family including me, my husband, and our sons and daughters all holding hands. Then I drew a group picture of each of my sons and daughters with their spouses, children, and pets. I labeled each person and pet by name. Then I wrote, "I remember . . ." in several places and added one of my favorite memories.

I left the markers in a tin box on her dresser. Taped to the lid, I included instructions encouraging other family members to draw pictures of their own families and then write their memories. The stick-figure families became quite elaborate, some with glasses, beards, bald spots, and hairstyles. The nurses and orderlies now had something to talk to Grandma about, and were better able to see her as a person. When they sat her out in the hallway with her quilt covering her, since her name was stenciled prominently in four-inch letters in the center of the quilt, even strangers walking by would greet her by name. Having everyone remind her of the happy times helped to raise her spirits.

Grandma died a few months after she entered the home, and I inherited her quilt. Whenever I snuggle into a chair with a book and her quilt over my lap, I feel surrounded by family, happy memories, and encompassed in her love again.

To use a quilt as a decorative wall accent, sew it with long sewing stitches to a weight-supporting fabric such as linen. A quilt can also be suspended from a self-adhesive Velcro strip or a Velcro strip that is stitched across the quilt's entire upper back edge. This enables it to bear the quilt's full weight. Attach to a supporting wooden strip on the wall. Never attach the quilt to the wall with tacks or nails.

Consult a folk art dealer, antique dealer, or professional quilt restorer for advice on the preferred way to hang a particular quilt style. Be aware that gravity can take its toll on a quilt that is hung for display.

■ ■ ■

The oldest quilted object known to man is a rug found in a Siberian tomb that may date from the first century B.C. It is also believed that the ancient Egyptians may have practiced quilting. Ancient carvings show objects that have a quilted appearance. The oldest known quilted objects from Europe include armor and whole cloth quilts from Sicily.

Blessed Be the Thread That Binds

LYNETTE TURNER

The thread on the spool of life began stitching its way through my family with my grandmother, who sewed out of necessity during the years when sewing for your family was less expensive than buying ready-made clothing. She lived with us in San Francisco as I grew up. Some of my favorite memories are of the after-school snacks that she prepared for me, including San Francisco sourdough bread and applesauce. Yum! After our snack, Grandma would play a game of checkers with me, but somehow she never won. She loved me so much and always invited me to join her, no matter what she was doing. Grandma loved to make doll clothes. She was a prim and proper lady and for that reason, the doll clothes were always sewn to the doll for which they were made so that they could not be taken off. I still have one of those dolls.

Continuing its work, the thread looped its way into my mother, who also had a passion for sewing. She not only made all of our clothes, she also made my wedding dress.

The thread stitched its way into my very soul when my father gave me a small Singer sewing machine. There I was, a five-year-old girl, sitting beside my mother. She would cut the material for her current project, take the scraps from the material, turn the edges under, and then iron the edges down. Then she handed the "scraps" to me so that I could sew on my machine while she sewed on her machine. As I stitched around the scrap with the only stitch that my little machine had, a chain stitch, my mother encouraged me to stay on the ironed edge. Even though my stitching was not straight all the time, my mother never touched it up. My father, a salesman, carried these pieces as his hankies. He was as proud as a peacock of these hankies, despite the fact that they were not square and had crooked stitching. My parents' attitude toward my abilities empowered me to be a lover of the craft of sewing today.

They say that you can tell if you are hooked on sewing if you have more than one machine. Today I own four machines and am considering a fifth. Like my grandmother and my mother, I made my children's clothes. The excess material from those clothes was piled up all over. A friend invited me to attend a quilting guild meeting with her to learn how to make good use of the excess material. I was a little skeptical at first because I thought quilts had to be made by hand and that quilters were generally in an older age group. Much to my surprise, the meeting was energized with enthusiasm. The participants were avid quilters of all ages focused on the completion of numerous projects. Many quilting techniques were being used. It seemed that there was no "wrong" way to accomplish a task. The greatest lesson I learned that day was that quilting by machine was perfectly acceptable. This positive atmosphere reminded me of my childhood and I was hooked. I have become so passionate about quilt making that I made fifty quilts in only one year!

As my grandmother helped care for me as a child, and my mother helped care for my children, so my husband and I helped care for my daughter's children. So it came to be that my youngest daughter, Kristi, and her husband, Anthony, came to live with my husband and me. To our delight, Kristi had her first baby while living with us. She and her husband took me along into the delivery room. After her baby was delivered, the doctor asked Anthony if he wanted to cut the baby's cord. Since this was his first experience, he felt unsure and squeamish. The doctor then turned to me, and I cut my grandson's cord. That was the beginning of a very special relationship between me and little Michael Valdez.

Michael and his parents lived with us for five years and we enjoyed caring for him while his parents were at work. My darling husband of thirty-five years, Bill, knew of my passion for sewing, and encouraged me to follow my dream of opening a home quilting business. He has been my biggest supporter and helped me change our house around to accommodate the eighteen-foot-long arm machine. My passion and this new business took me to the sewing machine every night.

Since the very beginning of his life, Michael sat with me. Early on, he would sit in his little seat and coo at me. When he learned to crawl, he found his way to the pile of warm, soft batting on the floor and sat in the middle of it while I machine quilted. Then he learned to climb and would climb right up on my lap to sit so he could have a better view of this process. When he got too big to retain his seat on my lap, he graduated to his own chair, right beside me. It seemed that he was content just to be near me. He observed me so closely that he soon learned what tool or supply I needed next and began to hand me what I needed without my even asking. My own children were not as interested in what I was doing as my little grandson was. His interest, contentment, sensitivity, and good nature endeared him to my heart.

When Michael was five, his dad received a much-anticipated promotion in the air force, based on his performance accomplishments. We were so happy for the family, but then our hearts sank when we heard that the promotion meant that Michael and his family would have to move to Italy and stay for three years. The move meant more separation between us than we had ever known.

When Michael found out that his family was moving, he asked me if I would make a quilt for him to take along. Because he watched me make quilts since he was very little, this seemed a natural request. Around that time I was attending a large quilt show, and discovered a book called *The Tamale Quilt* by Jane Tenorio-Coscarelli. Michael's paternal grandparents are of Spanish descent. In line with Valdez tradition, Michael's Spanish grandma would make tamales at Christmastime and Michael really loved going to his grandma's house for this special treat. So I began reading this book and I told Michael all about the quilt as I read. The pattern called for brightly colored *T*'s (for tamales, *and* my last name is Turner), olives (which my family loves), hearts (for love), and corn still on the cob with the husk pulled down (cornmeal is used to make tamales). A tamale quilt seemed to be such a perfect way to tie the two families together in a portable way for Michael to take to Italy. Grandma Valdez made the tamales and I quilted! With much enthusiasm, I started the "Tamale Quilt." Michael watched, as he always did, and asked with regularity, "Is it done yet?"

Each corner holds an appliquéd tracing of his hand and my hand. A personal adjustment to the pattern placed the olives in different arrangements on the fingers of the hands to help Michael learn how to count. As I sent Michael off to Italy, I told him that if he ever got lonely, to go sit in the middle of his tamale quilt and wrap it around him. When he did this, I told him that he would feel his grandparents back home placing their arms around him, hugging him up tight.

Quilting is truly the language that transcends any language, because it is the language of the heart.

When choosing fabrics:

■ *Intersperse white, cream, yellow, and any bright colors equally throughout the quilt design for a balanced look.*

■ *Choose a main print or pattern first before selecting coordinating solid colors and prints.*

■ *View fabrics near a window or take them outdoors to see their true colors.*

■ *For most quilts, a neutral fabric with a slight textured appearance makes a more interesting background than a solid white fabric.*

■ *Open the fabric on a bolt to a single layer when viewing. Since the fabric is in two layers, the shade may appear different when wrapped around the bolt.*

■ *Try using the wrong side of the fabric as the "right" side if you want the pattern to have a more subdued look.*

■ *Lay chosen fabrics out on a flat surface; take a step back to see how they look together. The beauty of a quilt design is inspired by the integration of all patterns, colors, and textures. This is usually best viewed from a short distance away rather than close up.*

A Special Gift

SIMONE MORTAN

Like so many new mothers, when my daughter Janine was born, I proudly sent out announcements of her arrival.

Upon receiving the announcement, Jenny, an old college friend, talked to her five-year-old daughter, Sarah Jane, about what they should send our new baby. Sarah Jane decided it would be nice to give the new baby something of her own. Jenny expected Sarah Jane to select a toy in which she had lost interest, but much to her mother's surprise, Sarah Jane selected the handmade green gingham quilt with appliquéd "Holly Hobby" figures she had received as a baby! "Mommy, this is my favorite blanket. I think it will keep the new baby nice and warm," reflected Sarah Jane. Jenny was torn between the desire to keep this memento of Sarah Jane's babyhood and the desire to honor her daughter's act of generosity. In the end, the caring child and her unselfish mother lovingly packaged the quilt and sent it to Janine.

Although Janine has never even met the generous little girl who sent her this gift, she has spent many nights on our living room couch cuddled under the quilt. When sleepover parties are planned, the quilt is carefully rolled up and placed inside her sleeping bag. The quilt has needed to be restitched a number of times, and the tag identifying its maker has long since fallen off.

Janine will graduate from high school this year. Although we have not yet talked about it, I have a sneaking suspicion that one of the items that will go off to college with her will be the soft, comforting quilt that she received as a baby — a reminder of unselfish love.

An investigation of wills and probate inventories from New England and the East Coast area shows that quilts were not common household items during the seventeenth and early eighteenth centuries. Blankets filled with corn husks or grasses and tied with twine passed as "quilts."

For ordinary families, fabrics were scarce. A high level of skill and many, many hours working on a spinning wheel or loom produced precious homespun fabric. Many hours were also needed to create homemade dyes.

The conditions of the time were not advantageous for creating beautiful quilt designs. Most quilts produced during these hard times were very plain and primitively designed, often being used until they fell apart or were recycled as linings for other bedding.

■ ■ ■

The sewing machine, created between the 1840s and 1850s, is one of the most important inventions to contribute to the growth and continuation of the quilting tradition.

Leslie's Healing Quilt

SARA FELTON

When Leslie Blair started working part-time at our fabric store, the Great American Quilt Factory, we were concerned about the number of commitments she had. How could anyone work full-time at one job, part-time at another, and raise a teenage daughter? Not only did Leslie prove us wrong, she quickly became a valued member of our staff. Even with all of her commitments, she was able to work a regular schedule, come to staff meetings, participate in monthly staff sew-ins, and hand make personalized cards for everyone's birthday. For our customers and us, Leslie was definitely a part of our quilting family.

It was shortly after Christmas when Leslie bravely shared the news with us. She had discovered a lump in her breast. Her doctors

160

determined that it was growing very quickly, and together they decided that the best treatment option was intensive chemotherapy to shrink the cancer, followed by a lumpectomy. We were scared for Leslie, who would be facing the horrors of this treatment. Our hearts were also with Leslie's daughter, Erin, who would have to grow up too quickly. And we were scared for *ourselves* — we didn't want to lose our new friend. We felt helpless and began looking for something that we could do to help.

Immediately we began to organize. We set up a schedule for giving Leslie rides to the doctor and delivering meals to her and Erin three days a week.

One day when Leslie was delivering a large stack of her handmade cards, someone said that since she made such beautiful cards, she would love to see her quilts. To our surprise, we learned that although she had been so generous with her creativity, she had never made a quilt. That's when we kicked into high gear. Chris, a friend and coworker of Leslie's, adapted a quilt pattern called "Love Letters" so that it could be worked with flannel. Nancy and Lynda, the shop owners, donated the wool batting. Susan, a long-arm machine quilter who works out of the store, volunteered to do the quilting.

Susan, another coworker, and her daughter researched healing colors and found that it would be best to make the quilt in pink, red-violet, blue-violet, blue, and violet. She made it clear that we *should not* use any green fabrics, because green is the color of growth and in this situation, we did *not* want growth. A night was chosen to hold a company quilting bee to make Leslie's quilt. Everyone raided his or her fabric stash before arriving. We worked together to select the fabric, design the pattern, and assign the color combinations. Then we began the ironing, cutting, and sewing, and after working late into the night, we had completed a quilt top. Within a week, Susan had added the backing and the stuffing and turned our creation into a quilt! She doodled with her machine to create a quilted secret garden of butterflies, flowers, and hearts.

The quilt was constructed using fifty-six eight-inch squares. Eight of those squares were envelope pockets randomly spaced around the quilt. The envelope blocks were made with the same fabric as the quilt, but had extra flaps of fabric that folded over and were able to be fastened, forming the envelope closure.

When the quilt was ready, we hid little treasures in the pockets for Leslie to open whenever she needed a little lift. The treasures included quotes on fabric like, "What counts is not necessarily the size of the dog in the fight, it's the size of the fight in the dog" by Dwight D. Eisenhower. We also included small cards, packages of candy, even chocolate Band-Aids! We also added a quilt label with a picture of us, and included all of our signatures. It read, "Here's a BIG warm hug from your friends at Great American!"

During her chemotherapy treatments, Leslie needed to be "socially recharged" and would come by to visit us at least once a week. One of our coworkers was driving Leslie around after one of her treatments, so we made sure to arrange a "visit." Leslie was beginning to lose her hair. Having always had long hair, she decided to have it cut short so it would be less noticeable. She was pale and weak. While it was difficult to see her like that, we were hoping our gift would lift her spirits.

The owners of our company, Nancy and Lynda, made the emotional presentation of our quilt. Leslie's eyes filled with tears when she opened the box covered with beautiful handmade paper. Ours did too.

Leslie has since told us, "It brings a smile to my face and warmth to my heart every time I wrap myself up in it. I draw strength from the love and devotion that was shared so well by all of these wonderful women, and friends — joys of my life."

Her ordeal is not over. She will soon be finished with her chemotherapy, and surgery to remove the tumor will follow. After that the future is unclear. We continue to keep our gift fresh by taking new treasures over to refill the pockets of the quilt that now rests on Leslie's couch, ready anytime she needs to wrap herself in our warmth, love, and friendship.

Generally, wedding quilts were all white and decorated with stitched twin-heart designs. Family and friends quilted the tops during quilting bees. The quilts were then used as part of a display created especially for the day of the wedding for the entertainment of the guests.

■ ■ ■

During the nineteenth century, some quilts in America were designed to remember a lost loved one. They were made in black or gray, decorated with appliquéd coffins or sewn from pieces of the departed one's clothing, and used as showpieces during the mourning period.

Stitched Together
with Love

CAROL RAVEN

In June 1992 my inner life shattered and I had no idea how to pick up the pieces. How does a middle-aged woman pick up the mirror-shards of life when every attempt cuts deeply? I didn't know. Neither did my husband, children, or friends. However, they believed in me, and gave me the strength to believe in myself.

Mary Jane Musson was a friend who believed.

For years, Mary Jane and I attended the same church and Bible study. We weren't close, just Episcopal church friends. I liked her accent, she liked my quilts. Old enough to be my mother, she seemed like a nice lady who had a strong connection to her faith. Young enough to be her daughter, I pretended to be connected.

Mary Jane believed in a God of loving tenderness. She believed in prayer, hugs, and listening without comment, advice, or interruption. She believed in caring. When my inner world shattered, I needed a mommy. She saw my need and mommied me.

She believed I could overcome the devastating effect of old emotional scars that limited me and made it hard for me to look forward to the future. She believed God loved me when I could not. She believed my tears would not — could not — go unshed. She believed I could cry myself whole in her arms as she rocked me through the sobs. She cared for me as she listened, prayed, cried, and challenged me. She shared her life with me, and gave me the courage to share mine with her.

Over the next two years, as our relationship deepened, my relationship with myself also deepened. I discovered who I was. I healed and became new.

As my journey into wholeness ended, Mary Jane's journey into death began.

One evening, alone together, I told Mary Jane about a book I had just read, *The Quilt*. In it, a dying matriarch had her family make her a burial quilt — a stressful task since time was short. Out of their combined efforts, a new family leader emerged — allowing the old woman to die in peace. I told Mary Jane that I had grown so much that I now believed in myself enough that I could become a leader. She leaned over, hugged me tight, and said, "Now I know it's going to be OK." Later that evening, Mary Jane told me that she was dying.

I cared for her as she had taken care of me. During the next six months I took her to the doctor, brought her food, drove her to church, and prayed with her. I made her a little quilt — six red paper-pieced hearts on a warm tan background. She hung it in her living room.

Over the years I had listened to her speak to me of living and now I listened while she was dying. Finally, I could only sit with her, as she became weaker and weaker. I watched her sleep. I watched her die.

Before she died she gave me a treasure as a tangible reminder of her love: a twin-sized double-wedding ring quilt that her mother had given her. I keep that gift in my sewing room. The quilt I had made as an expression of my love for her was returned to me the day of her funeral by her daughter-in-law. It now hangs in my living room.

Because of her loving care for me, I became strong enough to fulfill the affirmation I had expressed to her so many months before. I became a leader. I am pastoral care coordinator at our church, where I arrange caring service to our members in need. I take Mary Jane's wedding ring quilt with me to church weekend retreats for show-and-tell as I share my story — Mary Jane's story — of love, hope, encouragement, and healing. I wrap myself in it when I become discouraged or begin to despair. While wrapped in her quilt, I feel as though all the love and care that she extended toward me again enfolds and strengthens me, enabling me to continue ministering to others. Sometimes I think about restoring it — replacing a worn piece here, removing a stain there. But then I remember that quilts, like people, have imperfections. Quilts age. Eventually quilts die. Sometimes their stories do not. Mary Jane's life continues to influence others. She is still loving others, through my service to our parish family, and people are still healing.

■ *Fabric used to make quilts should always be prewashed. Wash the fabric in the same manner that the quilt will be washed. Be sure to dry the fabric in a dryer on the permanent press setting.*

■ *To check the fabrics for bleeding, soak bright or dark fabrics in warm or hot water in a small basin or sink first. To help prevent the fabric from fading and bleeding, soak it in a solution of one-half teaspoon Epsom salts to one gallon of cold water. Rinse well in warm water, and dry by hanging on a line outdoors or in an electric dryer.*

■ *If a fabric does bleed, wash it several times until the rinse water runs clear, then soak for half an hour in a tub of water that contains one cup of vinegar to each gallon of water to set the remaining color. These fabrics should be rinsed thoroughly twice.*

■ *Always prewash your fabrics before storing them. Then you will be able to start immediately with a newly designed project and you won't forget which fabrics have been prewashed and which haven't.*

The Fruitful Tree of Life

MARY MAYFIELD

It was Christmas Eve and we were gathered at Mom's old house, now owned by my daughter and her husband. Mom was in remission from cancer and living in a high-rise senior citizens center. She had lost a lot of weight, but at eighty years old, was still an attractive woman. Crippled with arthritis, Mom found it very difficult to walk, stand for more than a few minutes at a time, or hold anything of weight.

However, her spirit remained undaunted and she never complained. With dogged tenacity, she forced her legs to carry her across a room. The doctor said she should be resting in bed eight hours a day but she continued to do as much as possible. She loved her family, especially the grandchildren. She took a lot of medicine that

171

made it possible for her to stay mobile and kept the pain level down.

Because of all her ailments, we weren't sure Mom was going to be able to join us for our traditional holiday celebration, but she did. You could just tell by the energy in the room that everyone was excited that she was in our midst. At dinner we had consumed the traditional oyster stew, sandwiches, fruit soup, and cookies. Now we were sitting around the tree, ready to open our gifts. One by one we opened the many boxes and expressed our appreciation. Though we appreciated our gifts, we were all anxiously waiting for Mom to open the last gift, in a simple department store box. Hour after hour I'd worked on it, hoping to have it finished in time for Christmas, but here it was, Christmas Eve, and still not finished. I decided to give it anyway, while the whole family was gathered around. I could always finish it after the holidays.

All eyes were riveted on Mom as she removed the tissue paper and pulled out the unfinished quilt top. There, sewn into a "tree of life," were reproduced photos from the tree's roots to the top of its foliage representing various stages of our parents' lives. Pictures of their parents, their baby pictures, and pictures from their youth formed the roots. Mom and Dad's engagement and wedding photos were on the first leaves of the tree. Continuing up the tree were photos of each of us as we were born. The tree even pictured special moments we had together as a family, like my father playing with us in the park. The photos continued up the trunk and out onto the branches, showing the growth of the family as each of us got married and had children of our own. It was indeed a "fruitful" tree.

Mom was speechless as she ran her hands over the quilt top. She savored each photo with her eyes and was especially drawn to the ones of my father, who was killed in an accident twenty years earlier. Seeing photos of him as he loved and cared for his family warmed all of our hearts. The room was filled with our laughter as wonderful memories came flooding back and we told our own personal stories inspired by the photos.

Mom passed away before I could add the borders and stitch the quilt. After she died, however, finishing it became a priority to me. Now, because of all the memories it contains, it is my most cherished possession.

CHAPTER 4

Language of Quilts

*A quilt is
a blanket
of love.*

A Long Way Home

KATHY LAMANCUSA

It was the third year in a row I was hired to speak for clients in Leeds, England. My husband, Joe, and I decided to bring our two sons, Joey and Jimmy, along so they could experience all the sites we had enjoyed on our last two trips. The boys were twelve and fourteen at the time, a perfect age to begin to enjoy different cultures firsthand.

We spent nine glorious, fun-filled days touring the country from London to Greenwich and up to Leeds. The boys were to fly back to the States while my husband and I stayed behind for my presentations. On the way to the airport on the morning of the boys' departure, our friend Ian dropped me off to prepare for the next day while my husband continued on with the boys and Ian in the car.

177

Ten minutes from the airport, their vehicle was hit head-on by a tractor-trailer rig with both vehicles traveling at seventy miles per hour. Each of the four passengers sustained severe injuries, and all needed surgery and constant care for several weeks. Ian was in the hospital a week for observation of a head trauma. He also had surgery on his hand. My husband and younger son, Jimmy, were released from the hospital two weeks after the accident to return to the States for additional care.

Joey and I stayed in England. He had been the most seriously hurt of all and he needed to regain his strength and mobility before attempting the long trip home. While he seemed to be recovering well, he continued to complain about pains in his back.

Three days later, after additional tests, I was told that Joey had suffered a spinal injury, which the doctors hadn't noticed when he was admitted at the time of the accident. They wanted to put him in a plaster body cast and have him remain in the British hospital for three months to recover. Having already spent a few weeks in the hospital, I could clearly see that their treatments and methods lagged far behind what I had been used to in the United

States. The nurses told me on numerous occasions that because their medical systems were run under nationalized health care, there was not enough money to stay current with the best forms of medical treatments. Much of what we consider routine here in the United States is not available everywhere in England.

I felt I needed to seek a second opinion on the best way to treat Joey's broken back. Upon consulting by phone with orthopedic surgeons back in the United States, it was finally determined that we needed to return to the United States so that Joey could receive the most advanced care available for his broken back. This was no easy task! No U.S. commercial airline will fly a spinal injury victim. Finally, through a British service we were able to book passage on British Airways, which made accommodations to transport Joey by erecting a scaffolding system above the seats that he could be safely strapped to. Additionally, we needed to be accompanied by a private nurse who continued to see to Joey's care and administer the proper medications. Added to that were the challenges of international travel and the transportation of several suitcases holding our family's clothing and souvenirs. Before long, several days of sleepless nights and long days of planning had passed.

Our day of departure finally arrived, and we flew from Manchester to London and then on to Chicago, where we hired a private air ambulance to fly us to Cleveland's Lakefront Airport. An ambulance picked us up and drove us to Rainbow Babies and Children's Hospital, where Joey was admitted, underwent several tests, and then, finally, was placed in a hospital room to rest, approximately thirty-six hours from the time we boarded the first plane.

We had excellent service on every leg of this marathon trip, but the stress and concern over the proper care of my son and his constant need for love and attention had definitely taken their toll on my mind, body, and spirit.

Once my son was settled into the room, the nurse took one look at me and said I looked like death warmed over. I assured her I was fine and wanted to stay by my son's bedside as I had done for the past four weeks since the accident. She left the room and returned a few minutes later with a slip of paper. Handing me the paper, she said, "I just called the Ronald McDonald House next door and they have one room left. Your son has a long road ahead of him and he is going to need your love and support every step of the way. You will be of no use to your son without taking care of yourself. I promise you I will be here for his every need tonight. You go get a good night's sleep so you can be mentally and physically ready for the rest of this journey to recovery." I tried to argue, but finally gave in, so exhausted that I realized she might have a point.

Leaving my son that evening was one of the hardest things I have ever had to do. I wanted to hold and hug him, not leave him alone in bed. As I walked to Ronald Mc-Donald House I realized it was about 2 a.m., and I felt guilty and lonely.

I reached the house and opened the door. The housemother was waiting for me with a huge smile and an even bigger hug. She checked me in, handed me my key, and pointed in the direction of the stairs to my room.

As I turned I saw them — the quilts! They were hanging on all the walls in the reception area. Each featured bright colors and interesting shapes. There were more quilts as I climbed the stairs and as I walked down the long hall to my room — it seemed like they would never end. Each one was different, yet beautiful. And each one spoke to me with the warmth of a virtual hug.

I opened the door to my room for the evening and saw more quilts on the walls, and one magnificent quilt on the bed itself. As I climbed under the covers I felt all the invisible hands that had designed and created this masterpiece tucking me in. For the first time in days, I slept deeply and awoke refreshed and ready to stand by my son's side as he faced the challenges of his surgeries and recuperation.

I had started a cross-stitch design on the original flight to England and continued stitching it at my son's bedside throughout the weeks of his recovery. I told him about the quilts and their effect on me and we decided to turn the cross-stitch design into the focal point of a quilt created especially for Joey.

Planning and discussing the quilt together was a welcome diversion from the surgeries, medications, and long hospital days that Joey endured throughout his many weeks in the hospital.

When I finally brought him home, I took him to the fabric store in his wheelchair to select the fabrics with me. Since the cross-stitch design was an underwater fish and coral scene, we decided to use deep blues and greens to make the log cabin–style quilt that he loved.

Planning, sewing, and quilting this covering for Joey was therapeutic for me. Not having been in the accident myself, I was the primary caregiver and motivator for the recuperation of all three of "my guys." The journey was tough on them and tough on me. Spending hour after hour stitching this quilt was just the medicine I needed to heal.

When it was finished, Joey wrapped himself in it and looked quite content. The quilt hugged and warmed him throughout his high school years and to this day remains on his bed at home, ready for him to return from one of the many mountain climbing or outdoor trips he now regularly leads or participates in. He has fully recovered, and it's hard to keep him home.

The quilt is a testament to his strong will in overcoming the devastating situation he found himself in. Throughout his recovery he needed the strength to heal — but also the warmth and healing power of the messages this quilt shared with him each night.

"*But how many passages of my life seem to be epitomized in this patchwork quilt . . . here is a piece of that radiant cotton gingham dress which was purchased to wear to dancing school . . . By this fragment I remember the gown in which I supposed myself to look truly angelic . . . Here is a piece of the first dress which was ever earned by my own exertions! What a feeling of exultation, of self-dependence, of self-reliance was created by this effort!*"

— ANONYMOUS MILL WORKER,
1840–1845

■ ■ ■

"*The simple pleasures of the every-day life of the colonists and their close touch with nature are reflected in their quilt-patch names. Great-grandmother had no movies, no automobiles, no airplanes, no radios; is it any wonder she wove her pleasure into patchwork quilts?*"

— CARRIE A. HALL
AND ROSE G. KRETSINGER,
The Romance of the Patchwork Quilt

Dreams of Peace

Anna H. Bedford

We tore the package open as soon as it arrived, shook out the "Country Love and Peace Quilt," and carefully smoothed it over our bedcover. My husband, Jerry, and I would sleep under it for only one night, then we would pass it on to someone else. Together we poured over the note that came with the quilt. It read:

This beautifully appliquéd quilt was stitched by Emma Fisher Byler of Logantown, Pennsylvania. Emma is an active member of the Old Order Amish, a group deeply rooted in peaceable ways of living and in sustainable agriculture.

People from all walks of life have taken turns sleeping under the quilt. In a world where eight hundred million people go to bed hungry every night, those who sleep under it dream of a world where hunger ends and peace prevails. Upon awakening, they sign their name on the quilt and write their thoughts in the accompanying Dream Book.

Jerry and I knew the journey of the "Peace Quilt" would end at the Heifer Project International Quilt and Craft Auction scheduled in Chicago that fall. It would ultimately travel around the world for six months, sometimes being hand delivered, sometimes being shipped, but always carrying instructions regarding its next destination. It visited the United States, Africa, and India.

Jerry and I work for Heifer Project, an organization that seeks to end hunger around the world through gifts of farm animals and training in sustainable methods of agriculture. These animals — water buffalo, llamas, goats, cows, chickens, and bees — are ambassadors for peace, enabling families to become self-reliant for food and income. They also provide recipients with the dignity of becoming a giver, as they pass on their gift animal's first female offspring to another family in need. If this "Peace Quilt" brought a good price at the auction, it would feed many hungry families.

Eagerly we read the names of those who had already slept under the quilt. Former president Jimmy Carter wrote, "We slept under this quilt after returning from a visit to Africa to work on peace in the Sudan. We dream of a time for these people of peace without hunger." An African wrote, "I dream about women with babies on their backs. In loud voices they say, 'Please don't forget us!' May God bless those who share with others, and the Lord teach people to share." Mahatma Gandhi's granddaughter wrote, "Grandfather said, 'We must be the change we wish to see.'" Eight-year-old Michael's question written in the accompanying book asked, "Can we take turns being poor?"

Others who slept under the quilt included actor Ed Asner; Senator and Mrs. Dale Bumpers of Arkansas; villagers in Uganda and Kenya who had received help from Heifer Project; representatives of the Food Summit in Europe; a university professor in Poland; a conservationist; an Episcopal bishop; a peasant farmer; a Chicago homeless person; and a government official. It was clear that people of different ages, nationalities, income levels, and religions shared a common passion.

I wondered what Jerry and I would write after sleeping under this quilt. Africa is dear to our hearts because we lived and worked in Kenya, East Africa, in the 1960s. We specifically chose December 12 to sleep under the quilt because it's Kenya's Independence Day. As we got into bed and wrapped our arms around each other that night, we were flooded by the memory of standing in Nairobi Stadium in 1963 with thousands of Kenyans shouting *"Uhuru!"* — meaning freedom, *"Amani!"* — meaning peace, and *"Harambee!"* — meaning "Let us work together in harmony!" as the colonial flag came down and the flag of their new nation was proudly raised.

A few years later, when our daughter was born, we named her Amani. Now grown, she lives in Nairobi helping the hungry. She was to be married there on this December 12 and we were not able to be there. So, in the *Dream Book* I wrote, "As Amani and Regginald begin their new life together, our prayer for them, as for all nations and people, is a peacemaking one: Let us work together in harmony! *Harambee!*"

The "Country Love and Peace Quilt"

was successfully auctioned, bringing six thousand dollars. Elaine Waxman purchased the quilt to honor her mother, Rev. Dr. Rhoda Peters, who had worked with Jimmy Carter on a mission project in 1996.

On a mission for world peace, a single quilt unified the hopes and dreams of people from many lands and did much to aid worldwide hunger relief efforts.

Light at the End of the Tunnel

The lives of the Perez family in Mexico were changed because of a cow named Fortuna, donated by the Heifer Project.

Before Fortuna, the Perez family worked for three dollars a day and found it almost impossible to survive. Through the training and livestock from the Heifer Project, they found that the key to progress was working together as a community to make a better life.

Heifer Project teaches the community how to manage and care for the livestock, develop their community, market their new commerce, and perform the necessary bookkeeping. A gift such as a cow produces thirty liters of milk a day to drink or sell and several calves over its lifetime to be traded, sold, or passed on to other needy communities. The income produced provides money for housing, schooling, and health care.

For more information, call the Heifer Project International at 1-800-422-0474 or visit the Web site at www.heifer.org.

A Personal Patchwork

MARY KOLADA SCOTT

Women make more of anything
*   than it is worth.*
We compose paintings from
*   trays of trapped lint*
And sew enduring quilts from
*   petty scraps of cloth.*

> — *from* On the Back Burner,
> *by Mary Kolada Scott*

Last night I put the last stitch in a quilt that took two women and about sixty years to make.

Originally it belonged to my maternal great-grandmother, Margaret E. Stockman Stewart, who first pieced the quilt top in the 1930s but never finished it.

Although unfinished, the quilt top was

passed to my grandmother, then to my mother, who resigned the heirloom to a drawer. "Someday I'll cut it up and give a piece to each of you," Mom told her six children. "You can make pillows out of the pieces." That drastic prospect appalled me. Like my great-grandmother and my grandmother, and unlike my four sisters and brother, I loved sewing. In my youth, my favorite jigsaw puzzle depicted an old-fashioned quilting bee. As a young woman, I took a quilting class that heightened my awareness of the craftsmanship of this family heirloom so that each time I removed it from the drawer, I appreciated it more. Like the biblical mother who begged King Solomon to give her infant to another woman rather than see any harm come to him, I beseeched my mother to give the quilt to one child instead of parceling it out. Mom reconsidered and gave me the cover for my birthday a few years later.

My son, George, who was seven at the time I started quilting my great-grandmother's quilt, asked how long it would take to finish. "About a year," I blithely but naively answered. In a perfect world, it might have taken a solid, concentrated year. I didn't know it then, but the stitches of my idyllic life were beginning to unravel, and the next nine years would not be spent focused on stitchery.

My mother's death halted my progress and I sank into a severe depression. The quilt represented loss to me, reminding me of my mother and her mother, who had died three years earlier. Who would rejoice with me when the quilt was completed?

With the help of a counselor and the passing of time, grief abated and I began to feel that there was good therapy provided in the satisfying heft of substantial cotton fabric on my lap, and tiny stitches taken daily that accumulated into large areas of finished pattern.

Then my fourteen-year marriage failed, and we were forced to sell our spacious house. A freelance writer, college student, and homemaker, I was suddenly displaced and had to find a "real job" with a steady salary and benefits. My son and I moved to a small condo, where I planned to hang the quilt someday to brighten the dark, dull stairwell leading to my loftlike dwelling.

Reflecting, I wondered what other travels and travails my quilt had seen since its origin in the Depression. I knew that after its ownership was transferred to my grandmother, she drove with my mother, my father, my six-month-old brother, and me from Chicago to California. We were moving because my father had nearly died from rheumatic fever and was told that he needed to live in a warmer climate. I thought of the similarity to quilts existing in pioneer days, when women crossed these same plains in wagons, often burying children who couldn't survive along the trail. Many of their quilts reflected the hardships that they endured, and losses that they mourned. I wondered what stories my quilt would tell of its makers, my great-grandmother and me.

Now, suddenly single, I spent evenings after work quilting and watching television with my son. It provided continuity when nothing else was stable or familiar. The unraveling of some of the stitches of my life was beginning to slow and I knew that I was beginning to find healing and serenity when I opted for needlework and a video over a date with "just any man." The man would have to be someone very special to compete with an heirloom.

Years passed and the quilt was more than halfway completed. Like my adolescent son, I could start to see how both of my "life projects" would look when my part was done. I found that I was about to embark upon another of life's projects when I met, fell in love with, and married a man who appreciates my hobby. During the long evenings while my husband was at work, I again found that my quilt was my faithful companion. It endured patiently as physical ailments, dimming sight, and painful arthritis began to slow my progress.

Time passing, now finding myself in my forties, and my son needing less of me, I began to become unsettled as I saw the completion of my quilt drawing near. What would occupy my time, my life, my lap, when the quilt and child rearing were done? I was reminded of the myth of Penelope, who was besieged by suitors when her husband was thought lost in the Trojan War. Never losing hope for his return, she put off making a decision among suitors by promising to select one after the completion of her needlework. However, each night she removed all the stitches she had placed that day. Unlike Penelope, I couldn't craftily pick out the stitches each night to prevent the intolerable and inevitable. Comfort came as I realized that I had to finish what I had started and that an empty nest meant there was room for growth in other areas.

Completing the final stitches, I spread my quilt over our bed. The pattern is fittingly called "Grandmother's Flower Garden" and seen in its entirety, the garden for which it was named bloomed, its seeds having been sewn six decades ago by my great-grandma.

Through the years, I have learned many lessons. My great-grandmother's legacy — the quilt — was my primer. The seeds of strength of character, endurance, foresight, patience, and faith were developed during these years of quilting. Like life, the quilt took shape one stitch at a time, one day at a time. There is a sense of accomplishment when I survey the quilt spanning our bed like a prairie, crossed step by painful step. I take immense pleasure in binding up the ends that were unraveling from the past. My foremother speaks to me, given voice through her creative passion.

There on our bed my husband and I made love under the tent of the quilt's soft cotton and then slept peacefully under its comforting cover — my great-grandmother never having had the same opportunity.

■ *Some quilters feel that the best fabric choice for a quilt project is a good quality 100 percent cotton. It is the easiest to pierce with the needle and offers the least resistance to stitching with a needle and thread.*

■ *Quilters also consider the thread density of a cotton fabric — the higher the thread density, the easier it is to stitch. To test thread density, hold cotton fabrics up to the light — the least amount of light that can be seen through the fabric demonstrates the best quality. This is similar to thread count for sheets. The higher the thread count, the better quality sheet.*

With Love

JUNE STEWARD

My Dear Precious Granddaughter, Joy,

Your mother asked me to create a quilt from the cross-stitched top layer that she made for you while you were still in her womb. She thought it would be nice to have both her work and my work in your quilt, showing how much both of us love you. I have just finished the last stitch.

I want to tell you the story of your quilt. Someday, perhaps when you have your first child, you will understand and cherish it. It is a story of tenderness, great love, and sacrifice; one that your mother may never tell you completely, for she hurts as she remembers. There are hearts all over your quilt and a double hearts border. So, dear Joy, as you hold your quilt and read its story, see how much you are loved!

We all ached with indescribable sorrow when your older sister, Esther, was taken from us after her birth. Because of the complications during delivery, which ultimately took Esther's life, your mother's body was injured. Soon your mother was expecting you and was confined to bed to await your arrival. Your mother, father, grandfather, and I prayed during those long days while we waited for you. As your mother waited, she carefully and flawlessly stitched this quilt top, lying propped on pillows so she could work.

When the time came for you to be born, complications arose. Your parents feared losing you as they had lost Esther. The doctor had to work quickly to save your life. Your father, grandfather, and I waited, agonized, and prayed. God comforted me through Psalm 128:6: "Yea, thou shalt see thy children's children . . ." After the crisis passed, you were taken to the neonatal care unit. Your mother, weak from the traumatic delivery, cared only to know if you were well. At the news of your safe delivery and healthy body, we all were overcome with joy — thus the reason for your name. There could be no other word to express our feelings.

Joy, you are truly God's gift to all of us. We all love you so deeply. The double heart border on your quilt represents your mother and your grandmother forever "binding" you in love. Let this quilt always remind you, not only of how much you are loved, but also of God's graciousness to those of us who loved you before you were born. He answered our prayers, allowing us to rejoice at your birth. We continue to rejoice and love you even more and more. When your mother was born, her birth was a miracle. She then saw a miracle in your birth. What must God have planned for you? May you always seek him, love him, and serve him. He is so worthy!

I read this poem about a quilt but I do not know its author.

Warm Thoughts

Love is a quilt . . . a quilt is love.
Both love and a quilt should be:
Soft enough to comfort you,
Straight enough to cheer you,
Generous enough to enfold you,
Light enough to let you move freely,
Strong enough to withstand adversity,
Durable enough to last a lifetime,
And given gladly from the heart!

So, precious one, we give you this quilt. Enjoy it!

Love,
Grandmamma

Use a color wheel for assistance when selecting coordinating fabrics for a quilt design. Knowing and using color schemes will help your selection process.

1. *A monochromatic color scheme uses tints and shades of one hue. It is considered to be the most pleasing of all color combinations. Begin with any color, such as red, and combine it with a tint (the color combined with white) such as pink, and a shade (the color combined with black) such as deep red to burgundy.*

2. *An analogous color scheme consists of one primary or secondary color and the colors that are near it on the color wheel. This color scheme is flexible and may include colors a step or two away from the original color.*

3. *A triad color scheme uses three colors that are equally spaced around the color wheel. Examples include: red, blue, and yellow; orange, green, and violet; or yellow-green, blue-violet, and red-orange.*

4. *A complimentary color scheme uses colors that are directly opposite each other on the color wheel. This represents a bold, vibrant color scheme. Examples include: blue and orange; red and green; or yellow and violet.*

The Day God Called You Home

PENNY BERENS

It was an ordinary July day for most, but, to me, it was the ghastly day I got a call informing us that my beautiful, twenty-one-year-old son, Steven, died on his way to work. The driver of the car that killed him had fallen asleep at the wheel.

For several months, I found solace in helping his father, two brothers, and the friends who came to visit cope with their grief. Helping others had made it easier for me not to face what I was personally feeling. Having all those young people around, sharing their feelings and stories about Steven, helped all of us to continue to feel connected to him by talking about him.

But I had other strong feelings. I felt as if my heart were literally broken in two. It was a real and very physical pain. Several weeks passed with me holed up inside my home before I simply had to go to the grocery store for food and supplies. I was dumbfounded that the world was carrying on as usual around me. I felt almost as if I were dishonoring my son by allowing my world to get back to normal. As I walked down the grocery aisles, I wanted to scream out that my son had been killed and I was hurting.

Over several months, there were many people to tell about Steven's death. And there came a time when I could not stand to see the shock and pain sweep across another person's face as he or she was told that Steven was no longer with us.

I needed to face my own grief. I began retreating to my favorite place, my sewing studio, a bright sunny room off my bedroom, every evening after work. I felt comfortable, safe, and free there. Having been brought up to keep my emotions in check all the time while putting on a brave face, I felt free to allow myself to feel pain. Allowing myself to really feel my grief was a new and scary thing to me. While there, I was surrounded by what felt "friendly" and familiar — my fabrics and thread.

I began to let my feelings come out

through the creative avenue of quilting. It is much easier for me to express my emotions through quilting than it is for me to do so through words. I allowed my raw feelings of anger and pain to take control. When I was creating in my studio, the times were sessions of pure grief over the loss of my son.

Originally, I did not go to my studio with the intention of making a memory quilt *celebrating* my son's life, but it did become vitally important while I was there to record that day in July and the effect it had on the people that I love. I felt compelled to name the quilt "The Day God Called You Home." This piece was not meant for others to see. Designing it was a very solitary and painful process.

The wall hanging that resulted from those quiet times shows a day that began bright and sunny, but was torn asunder by a streak of lightning that sapped all the color out of our lives. The left-hand side of the quilt depicts a cheerful, crazy-patched, and embroidered world surrounded by the Celtic "tree of life" design. On the dark side of the wall hanging, the car is coming toward us. For some reason, it was important that there was not a figure of a driver in the car, but the embroidered *Z*'s symbolize the fact that he was asleep.

There is a dove soaring upward, carrying Steven's heart and the keys to the doors of heaven. A snuffed candle symbolizes the end of his promising future, and a cross represents his tombstone. Hands pull gray fabric back, and reveal color again representing the love and support of our friends and neighbors. Of course, it will never be as bright as the color at the beginning of the day.

With trepidation, I showed the finished quilt to my family. To my surprise, they requested that it be hung in the front hall, where I often saw them touch it as they passed by.

After sharing "The Day God Called You Home" with the family, I felt that it helped all of us to heal. This motivated me to share it with others. As a result, it tours with me when I am asked to speak at quilting guild meetings about using our passion for quilting to help us heal from our hurts as well as celebrate our joys.

I owe my sanity and the ability to carry on to the love and support of the three special men left in my life, and also to the creative process of quilt making.

■ *The creation of a quilt sometimes enlisted the skills of an entire family. Children and older female members would cut the fabric pieces and thread needles, while husbands would cut pattern templates or draw patterns on a quilt top.*

■ *Appliqué is the process of adding cut pieces of fabric to a fabric base. It can be taken a step further by adding materials such as beads, shells, metals, and jewelry.*

Countless Names

BILL GARDNER

I first saw the NAMES Project AIDS Memorial Quilt in Washington, D.C., in 1988. It is not your typical quilt: It's made up of thousands of individual three-by-six-foot panels and commemorates the lives of thousands of men, women, and children whose lives have been lost to AIDS.

In 1988 the quilt included 8,300 panels. Today there are more than 44,000. You can imagine, even with just 8,300 panels, how big this quilt was. It's pieced together so there are walkways between blocks of panels, allowing viewers to see each panel up close and personal.

The experience of seeing the quilt for the first time was deeply emotional for me. I cried a lot. In fact, it was difficult to spend more than just a few minutes viewing the quilt before my eyes filled with tears again. Thankfully, organizers placed boxes of tissue next to each block of panels.

Although there were thousands of people there, it was a quiet, dignified, and respectful crowd. As visitors toured the quilt, readers read the names of the deceased. Hearing the names also broke my heart, especially when someone would end a reading with, "And my dear friend . . ."

The quilt panels varied in designs. Some were simple, some complex. I remember seeing pieces of the deceased's clothing incorporated in a number of ways. There were photos, there were letters. One letter was written to the deceased and described the memorial service high atop a mountain where friends and family had gathered to scatter the ashes. "You would have been proud of your mother," the letter said. "She handled it so beautifully."

Some panels were humorous. Some were dignified. Each honored the dead in its own way. The last time I saw the quilt on display in its entirety was in 1993. This time I went with friends. Our group of friends was there to deliver a panel to which we all contributed. The panel had been created in honor of a loved one, "D," a member of our group who had died. The panel was beautiful. It was a tribute to "D"'s love of Christmas. We found we couldn't part with the panel, though — at least not then. Instead, we laid it out on the ground and we all sat around it and reflected. While we talked, we cried, and we laughed. Others came by to view this new panel and also wept openly. During this intimate time we remembered "D" and how kind, thoughtful, and loving he was. While we mourned his loss, we also celebrated his life.

The quilt panel helped us. It helped us mourn and it helped us celebrate. In fact, it is very clear that the NAMES Project AIDS Memorial Quilt helps everyone who has lost a loved one to AIDS do the very same.

The Heart of the Matter

DEBBI LIEBERSON

Many times during the months he was sick, I thought about asking my husband, Rich, what he would want on his panel for the AIDS quilt. But I never found a way. More than a year after his death, I began working on a project that I thought would feel safe and familiar, that would help me begin my healing. Sewing and quilting had been part of my life for years, and I looked forward to creating a tangible memorial that would show the times before AIDS, before pain and ugliness overgrew so much of our lives. I wanted people to know about Rich's politics, and his humor, and his love for our son, Ben.

Several weeks after he died in 1991, I donated all of Rich's clothing to a shelter for homeless men. All except his T-shirts. Those I meticulously folded into a large cardboard box that I put on the top shelf of my bedroom closet. Some of his shirts were so worn that they barely held together. Every one displayed a message: "Free Nelson Mandela," "Peace in a United Ireland," "U.S. Out of El Salvador." Each was laden with memories of demonstrations Rich participated in, articles he had written, political arguments we had had.

One evening the following winter, I cleared a large area to begin my work. I spread out the three-by-six-foot piece of black fabric I planned to use for the background. This size had been specified in the literature I received from the NAMES Project, the organization that sponsors the AIDS quilt. Only later did I learn the significance of the dimensions. Each quilt panel is the size of a gravesite.

For the first time, I opened the box of T-shirts I had packed up so many months before. I smelled each one as I unfolded it, covering my nose and mouth with the fabric. Each time, I breathed in slowly, hoping to capture one last time something of the Rich I loved. Not the smells of his sickness and his dying, but the cucumber-celery smell of his sweat that had intoxicated me when we made love, years before. I felt cheated when I realized that every shirt smelled exactly the same. The floral-scented laundry detergent was unfamiliar. I wondered which of our friends had done these last loads of laundry for us.

For hours on that day and in the weeks to come, I played with those T-shirts, along with photos, political buttons, and memorabilia of all sorts. I lined objects up with symmetry and precision, then scattered them randomly. I balanced splotches of brightly colored fabric and then added more muted tones. I overlapped, rearranged, made sketches on graph paper. Nothing I did looked right. I hated every design I created.

One rainy afternoon, weeks later, I realized I was no closer to completing a quilt than when I'd unpacked Rich's T-shirts. Angry and frustrated, I refolded and repacked each one and put the box back on the top shelf of my closet. Months later, I went to see a display of a small portion of the AIDS quilt at a local university. Along with hundreds of other people, I wandered among the panels. Every few minutes I would hear a Kleenex being pulled from one of the many boxes placed throughout the room. Quiet sobs punctuated the silence. Once a young man cried out loudly, unwilling or unable to modulate his grief.

Some of the panels were elaborate, stunning works of art. Others were almost childlike in their simplicity. I returned home that day knowing that I had to make a quilt panel for Rich.

This time I took a completely different approach. I visualized colors and abstract forms. I drew shapes in peacock blue, indigo, violet, aqua, the colors I love. The black background made the colors vivid and alive. Inspired, I worked with renewed energy and excitement until I realized what should have been obvious. I was designing a quilt for myself. It was capturing my personality, my spirit. I knew, even if no one else would, that what I was looking at had nothing at all to do with Rich. The revelation and my total resignation came simultaneously. I would not make a quilt for Rich. Ever. That I didn't understand why made the decision no less immutable. AIDS had won, again.

Ben walked into the room just as I finished cleaning up. He looked surprised. "Did you finish Iggy's quilt?" (Iggy was the name Ben had given Rich when he was a baby, just beginning to talk.)

"Nope."

"How come?"

"I don't know. I just couldn't figure out how to make it."

For months, Ben had seen me working. I could tell by the look on his face that my five-year-old was confused by my giving up, with nothing to show for all my time. Without giving the question any thought, I asked Ben, "Do you want to make a quilt for Iggy?"

"Sure."

It was so easy for Ben.

"I want it to be mostly red." Red was Ben's favorite color.

"What do you want it to say?"

"Iggy was my dad. And we used to play guitar together and Iggy would write silly songs about me. And I want it to have a picture of me and Ig together. And I want some stars and some moons and a giant zigzag line, like lightning. Can we go to Pearl Art and get gold and silver paint? Or maybe they have glow-in-the-dark paint."

The next day we went shopping for Ben's supplies. When we got home, he was ready to begin work.

"I'll show you where to put my words. Make sure you write real light, so no one will see your letters after I paint over them. OK, Mom?"

Ben's bold, unself-conscious strokes with a large paintbrush filled much of the center of the red cloth. He proudly painted "Iggy was my dad" in wonderfully garish gold paint. Without a word of discussion, he grabbed another brush and dipped it into the white paint. He surrounded his letters with large, randomly placed blobby dots.

Later that day, we sat down with our photo albums. With great seriousness, Ben turned page after page and then announced decisively, "I want this picture, and I want this one on my quilt."

We called a number of places until we found one that would copy our photos directly onto our fabric. Rainbow Visions normally transferred photos onto T-shirts in quantities of a dozen or more. But when I explained that we were making a panel for the AIDS quilt, the man did not hesitate. "Why don't you bring your stuff over right now?"

Ben's questions were nonstop. He was fascinated by the machines and photographic equipment at the workshop.

"So how do you get the paint from the machine onto the T-shirt? And how do you do it so all the colors of wet paint don't smear all over the place? And, wait a minute, how did you get that picture on a shirt without taking it out of the magazine?"

One man spent nearly an hour with Ben answering his questions and demonstrating each gadget they encountered on their tour of the studio. We left with more copies of our photos than we needed and with Ben wearing a zebra T-shirt made from a picture in *National Geographic* that was still in the magazine.

Less than a week after he had begun, Ben's work was done. Unlike anything I had attempted, his quilt captured Rich's spirit. We took his panel to the local chapter of the NAMES Project. Ben looked proud, and he listened attentively as one of the volunteers explained what would happen next.

"Your panel will be packed up with several others and sent to California. There it will be photographed and given a number. That way, if you ever want to find out where it is, you can."

The woman paused for a moment and then wondered out loud, "You know, it is possible that you're the youngest, or at least one of the youngest people, to make a panel for the AIDS quilt."

Ben smiled.

Ben, of course, had no way to know what his making a quilt panel for Rich meant to me. This small boy, with a wave of a paintbrush, effortlessly beat back a tyrannical demon I was powerless to move.

All these years later, I still am grateful.

In 1985, Cleve Jones, an activist, organized and participated in a candlelight march. He had learned that more than one thousand of his fellow San Franciscans were lost to AIDS. Overwhelmed by this realization, he asked each of his fellow marchers to write the names of friends and loved ones who died of AIDS on placards. At the end of the march, Cleve and others stood on ladders and taped the numerous placards to the walls of the San Francisco Federal Building. When completed, the wall looked like a patchwork quilt. Inspired by this sight, Cleve and his friends made plans for a larger memorial. A little over a year later, he created the first panel for the AIDS Memorial Quilt in memory of his friend Marvin Feldman. In 1987, the NAMES Project Foundation was formally organized.

Response to the quilt was immediate and people from several large cities that were most affected by AIDS began sending quilt panels to the San Francisco workshop. The project has grown and now thirty-six countries have contributed panels to the quilt.

Today, there are 34.3 million people worldwide living with AIDS (17.3 million men, 15.7 million women, and 1.3 million children under the age of fifteen). More than half of those infected are not being treated. An alarming amount of HIV-positive women do not even know that they are infected.

The quilt is a powerful, visual reminder of the AIDS epidemic. There are more than 44,000 panels. Each panel is three feet by six feet — the size of an adult grave — and commemorates the life of someone who has died of AIDS. Sadly, this vast number of panels represents only a very small percentage of those who have died from AIDS.

If laid end to end, the three-by-six-foot panels would span fifty miles. Side by side, the panels would completely cover sixteen football fields, totaling more than 792,000 square feet. The whole quilt weighs more than fifty tons.

The last viewing of the entire quilt was in October 1996 in Washington, D.C. The quilt spanned the entire length of the Mall, from the Capitol Building to the Lincoln Memorial. Because the epidemic continues to claim more lives, and more panels are made, the quilt has grown too large to display in its entirety. Although there are no plans for future displays of the entire quilt, the planners are dedicated to displaying as much of the quilt as possible around the world so that more people can experience it.

According to research by the U.S. Depart-

ment of Health and Human Services, an average of at least one American under the age of twenty-two becomes infected with HIV every hour of every day. Twenty-five percent of the forty thousand Americans who are newly infected with the HIV virus every year are thirteen to twenty-one years old. The majority of these young people are infected by sexual contact.

According to the Centers for Disease Control, there were 733,374 cases and 430,441 deaths reported through December 1999 in the U.S. alone. The mission of the NAMES Project is "to use the AIDS Memorial Quilt to help bring an end to the AIDS epidemic." Its goals are to provide a creative means for remembrance and healing, to illustrate the enormity of the AIDS epidemic, to increase public awareness of AIDS, to assist with HIV prevention education, and to raise funds for community-based AIDS service organizations. The project has raised more than $3 million to date.

The AIDS quilt has redefined the tradition of quilt making. It is a memorial, a tool for education. It is a healing response to the tragic loss of human life.

For more information, please visit the AIDS Memorial Quilt Web site at www.aidsquilt.org.

■ ■ ■

The Magic Quilt

ISABELLE CARLSON

About six weeks before my daughter was due to have her first child, I started making a quilt for the baby. One week later, Erika went into labor prematurely and gave birth to Kelvin Watson Jr. Although Kelvin was a very healthy size at six pounds, he was still a very sick little boy. His lungs were underdeveloped, and at birth he was whisked into the intensive care unit. His prognosis was grim.

Visitors were restricted so I was unable to see my grandson more than once. I ached to hold him and talk to him. I was terrified that we would lose him. To calm myself, I turned to the quilt that I had started for him the week before, but I felt afraid to start working on it again. What if Kelvin didn't make it? Would this quilt become a reminder of the family's loss? In the midst of my fears, needing something to occupy my mind, I picked the quilt up and started working on it again.

Working on Kelvin's quilt was so comforting — it was almost as if I were holding him and communicating with him. Each stitch was an expression of the depth of my love.

Still fearing the worst, I continued to work on the quilt for my comfort. One month after he was born, Kelvin left the hospital. But the quilt was not yet finished. We were so happy he had recovered — I wanted to do the quilting by hand so it could be perfect for him. My daughter, wanting to have the quilt for her new baby, asked about it often. Reevaluating the time that it took to hand quilt, I finally decided to do the quilting by machine. Finally finished when he was a year old, I gave him his quilt.

As he grew, he also grew to love his quilt. He even took it to kindergarten with him. He took it to show-and-tell in first grade, and told his schoolmates that this quilt was made especially for him.

Kelvin is now ten — as healthy and energetic as any of his playmates. The special blanket now resides in his room and we call it the "magic quilt" because he tells us he feels safe when he has it.

It warms my heart to hear him say, "Grandma, every time I see my magic quilt I want to wrap myself in it because I can just feel your love and hugs!"

"Because of the written words and needlework skills of our ancestors, we can travel through time and share their good times and bad, plenty and want, joy and sadness. Through it all, we feel a kinship and a sense of heritage because we have quilting, too."

— PAT MAIXNER MARGARET
AND DONNA INGRAM HUSSER

■ ■ ■

Sustained by a Thread

SARAH JANE MCMILLEN

The individual moments of our lives are connected with the thread that runs through them. My life is woven with experiences of exceptional love and inexpressible sadness. I have been blessed with heroes, champions, life and death, love and selflessness. Through every tear, an invaluable faith and the comfort that quilting brings have been the threads that have sustained me.

When I married Ray, we could never have known the events that were to shape our lives. After having three children — Steve, Jeff, and Michael — Ray attended Indiana State College in our hometown of Terre Haute. While there, my four-year-old, middle child, Jeff, was diagnosed with leukemia. The day before Jeff died, my youngest, Michael, was found to have a malignant tumor on the nerve lining in his back.

This diagnosis bewildered the doctors — two boys in the same family with two very different forms of cancer? Michael was sent to specialists in Cincinnati. While I stayed with him there, my mind was overwhelmed with worry about what was happening. I needed something to take my mind off the constant worry. I turned to one of my passions, quilting, for comfort. I found that quilting not only helped me personally, but it helped me to be there for Michael. Before I started quilting, he could see the constant worry in my eyes. After I started quilting my thoughts were no longer totally consumed with the worst.

Several surgeries and radiation treatments for Michael necessitated a long stay in Cincinnati. Ray continued his schooling back in Indiana and his parents helped him care for our oldest son, Steve. Staying at the hospital with Michael, I met many other mothers whose children were undergoing similar treatments. They saw how quilting helped me to cope and several decided they wanted to learn. I brought fabric, needles, and thread and began to teach them to piece quilt squares. Helping others in need served as a valuable respite for me and helped fill the hours until Michael recovered and we were able to go home.

After Ray finished his education, we moved to Florida, where he began to work as a police officer. A year later Ray passed out at the wheel of his cruiser. The doctors found no cause for the blackout and decided that it was due to the stress we had experienced during our sons' illnesses.

A few months later, my oldest son, Steve, began complaining of pain in his leg. Being the eternal optimists, we assumed that he had only pulled a muscle. Doctors found a tumor in the apex of his bone and his leg had to be amputated. Again, I started quilting.

Now, with three sons having different types of cancer, the media became involved. Steve was very courageous and determined to recover. Throughout his treatments, he was interviewed often and loved being "center stage."

After his recovery, we decided that a family vacation was just what we all needed, so we bought a used motor home and headed out west. Starting in Miami, Florida, we decided we would go as far as we could on half of our money and when that was gone, we would turn around and head for home. To our surprise we made it all the way to Mount Rushmore, South Dakota, where we camped at a campground at the base of the mountain.

One day while we were enjoying the beauty of the area, Ray became worried about our dog. He left to check on him in the motor home at the campground. We watched as he walked down the road and then we continued sightseeing. It seemed like a great deal of time had passed, but Ray did not return. The boys and I became worried and went to look for him. As we walked down the road to the campground, we saw a crowd milling around someone lying on the ground. As we approached, I could clearly tell that the person on the ground was Ray. Emergency vehicles arrived and transported us to the hospital. The doctors were concerned with the test results and suggested we get Ray back home as quickly as possible and into a hospital with the proper equipment to diagnose his illness. We made it back to Florida in only three days as I drove the old motor home filled with our two kids, a dog, and a very sick husband.

After numerous tests, the doctors found a brain tumor. Now we were in shock. How could this be? All three sons and my husband were all diagnosed with different types of cancer. It baffled the doctors and the National Institutes of Health became involved. We transported Ray to the institute in Maryland, where the doctors removed the tumor and radiation treatments began. I again took up quilting.

Ray actually recovered very well and we returned to Miami, where he went back to work.

Meanwhile, Steve went off to college and thrived, becoming student body president and leading a busy life. After graduation, he attended law school.

Our journey with cancer didn't seem to be over, though. Back at home, Michael developed pain in his legs and the doctors discovered bone cancer. The surgeries were extensive and the ordeal eventually put him in a wheelchair. He bravely faced this new challenge, but I was getting close to the end of my rope.

I began to make promises to God. I promised that I would go to church every time the doors opened, that I would be the kind of Christian that I knew I ought to be — *anything!* I just asked that he please let me keep my children. Through this introspection I learned that you cannot bargain with God. God is in control. I was led to look at what I had. I had been blessed with a loving husband and three wonderful children. The time that we shared together was real quality time. I saw that what I had was *really* special.

But our journey wasn't over. Ray developed a problem with his hand and had trouble remembering words. The doctors found that there was another tumor, but this time, it was on the opposite side of his brain. It was a different tumor! This new development helped the doctors finally figure out the mystery. The reason that all four of the men in my life developed cancer was because they were radiation sensitive. Any radiation — even from a tooth X ray — was lethal to them and caused cancer to develop. For most people radiation is not dangerous, but the very thing we did to try to kill their cancers created more cancer. From that time on, none of them had any more radiation.

Michael was in the hospital in Cincinnati at the same time that I was with Ray when he was having his second brain tumor removed in Maryland. When Ray came out of his surgery, I got the call that the doctors in Cincinnati found that Michael's malignancy had spread to his lungs. For the next several days, I spent most of my time on an airplane between the two. Michael died three days later. Ray died seven weeks after Michael. Through it all, I quilted.

Steve's spirit remained strong. He graduated from Oxford and took three months to backpack through Europe on his one remaining leg. After his adventure, he returned home, developed a law practice, and was invited to be on the Orange Bowl committee. He loved life, was healthy, strong, and brave.

Seven years had passed since Ray died and I met and married a wonderful man named Bert.

One day Steve collapsed on the baseball field while playing with his firm. The doctors found a brain tumor. Learning of this overwhelming discovery, I decided just quilting a project wasn't enough. I had to do something to reflect the feelings that I experienced throughout my life. I began to quilt an album quilt, a design where each block denotes an event in life. The quilt I made reflects about thirty years of emotion. It reflects my marriage to Ray and the births of our three sons. It reflects the emotions through our hospital days. It reflects my marriage to Bert. It also denotes hurricane Andrew, which wiped out our home shortly after we were married. The quilt signifies that during every moment of stress in my life, I turned to the comfort of quilting. It reflects every piece of me. I needed to create this in order to keep life's celebrations and challenges in balance.

Steve worsened and came home to live with me before he died. One day I said to him, "I am so sorry that I brought you into this world of suffering." Steve summed it up so beautifully when he replied, "No! It was worth it! It's the quality of life! Quantity isn't important! Some people live until one hundred years old and don't have a wonderful life!"

Steve died June 10, seventeen years to the day, and almost the hour, after Michael died. Each of my sons and my husband understood how to find the joy in life and each lived their life to the fullest. They had no regrets and that's what matters.

For me, quilting has been a healing force. My stitching has started and stopped as our problems came and went. Through all of the challenges we experienced my faith in God and my quilting were the threads that sustained my life.

■ *Historically, when patchwork quilts were new they were first used for guests and then by the master and mistress of the household. After they became worn they were handed down to the servants and may have ended up in the barn as a blanket for a horse.*

■ *In Sweden and Holland, patchwork quilts were associated with simple people, often referred to as "poverty covers" and "beggars' covers."*

■ *Buy extra fabric — at least one-half yard of each pattern — to cover errors, and if you know that you will be working on your project for a while. Fabric selections in the stores are sometimes discontinued seasonally. Be sure to purchase more than you think you will need. You can use any extra fabric for scrap quilts if you don't use it all for your main project.*

Threads of Time

DEB HOPKINS

In my lifetime, the creation of quilts and the act of giving those quilts as gifts have provided me with the pleasure of communicating with people in a very special way. What some people do not understand, however, is that sometimes the quilts themselves speak out. The language that these quilts speak is a silent one that is translated into the emotions that we feel when we know the story behind the quilt. For as long as I live, I shall never forget creating two special quilts. The story behind these two quilts reached out, tugged at my heart, and brought tears to my eyes.

A tragic airline accident took the lives of a husband and his two children. His wife was left alone, carrying his unborn child. Though I never met this family, my heart ached for this unintentionally abandoned expectant mother. A friend asked me to put together two quilts for the mom-to-be that were to be given by her as gifts. They were to be constructed from some of her husband's jeans. The first of the two quilts was to be for his unborn child, the second, for his parents.

It was both a pleasure and a torment to complete these quilts. As I began to work with the fabric, different feelings flooded my heart. Sometimes a sense of sadness would come over me as I realized the circumstances and the importance behind the task I had undertaken. Upon completion, I stretched the quilts on the floor for one final look before shipping. As I gazed upon the "comforters" and reflected upon those who would receive them, deep sympathy was forever etched in my heart and mind. It was my friend's account that enabled me to be a part of the presentation of the quilts to the family. My friend's words depicted the tears and emotion felt by all. I experienced a connection with the family even though I will probably never meet the people to whom these quilts belong.

The gift of a quilt is a timeless one — one that never grows old and one that never tires. A quilt holds the true spirit in which it was given down through the ages. I call that gift "The Threads of Time."

■ *When using a sewing machine for quilting, change the needle after forty to fifty hours of sewing. Dull needles leave larger holes in your fabric and disturb the machine's tension. A burr on a needle will catch the fabric's fibers, causing it to pucker as well as causing thread to break or get fuzzy while stitching.*

■ *Ultraviolet light can be very damaging to quilts. You may want to replace glass in doors or windows of a room where a quilt is displayed with a UV-filtering glass or Plexiglas, or cover with a UV-filtering shield or a Mylar polyester film.*

■ *Fluorescent light fixtures can also be fitted with special filtering sleeves or shields.*

■ *Store quilts in the same climate that is comfortable for you. Extreme temperature changes, dampness, or humidity can be detrimental. Good air circulation is also important to reduce the chance of mold or mildew forming.*

Heaven's New Star

MARY COLLINS

In rare and sweet circumstances, we form an uncommon bond with the people who are brought into our life. That uncommon bond is one of freedom. Freedom to laugh, freedom to cry, freedom to be ourselves. When fate tears those friendships apart, the void left is a chasm deep and wide. Such was the friendship formed with Kyle Miller, who was shockingly ripped out of my life when his flight from New York's Kennedy Airport bound for Paris's de Gaulle Airport crashed ten miles off the shores of Long Island on July 17, 1996, just fourteen minutes after takeoff.

I met Kyle while remodeling our home earlier that same year; he was brought in as our plumber and electrician. The reconstruction process requires plumbers and electricians to spend many hours and sometimes many weeks on the job. Since this job was in my home, Kyle and I got to know each other well. When someone is in your home many hours, many days, it is natural to strike up conversations. Sometimes we talked between rooms, other times in passing, and as time wore on, our conversations became deeper as we found a natural friendship forming. We especially enjoyed each other's humor.

There were times that Kyle had to come to our home at six or seven o'clock in the morning to resolve plumbing and electrical emergencies. When these situations arose, I felt a little embarrassed as I opened the door because usually I was just out of bed, dressed in a bathrobe, and definitely not yet ready to face the world. My hair was very unruly, and my face hadn't seen an ounce of makeup. Kyle endeared himself to me by seeing the humor in the situation. He would just come in with a smile and a tongue-in-cheek comment like, "Well, Mary, you're looking lovely this morning." Whether emergency or "normal" working conditions, it was fun to have him in our home. When he walked in things seemed better. We were always able to laugh together.

That fateful day he was on his way to Paris with his wife, Amy, in celebration of their fifth wedding anniversary. From the day that I learned of Kyle's fate, I felt I needed to make a memorial quilt. It was my way to grieve his death. But because I was so sad, I couldn't work on it for a long time. I didn't finish it until May 2000.

Originally I thought I would give the quilt to Kyle's parents, but I can't seem to part with it. Hanging in our home, it brings sweet memories of his presence there. Even so, I feel in my heart that I am now ready to share the quilt with others.

In the center of the quilt, there stands a tree of life in the form of a weeping willow, barren of its leaves. The leaves lie in a big pile beneath. Each leaf is cut from a different fabric to symbolize the uniqueness of each of the 230 lives lost in this crash. Surrounding the tree are 228 stars representing the lives lost but not forgotten. There are two more stars — Kyle's star is the largest and is right next to the star that represents his wife, Amy, placed in the sky, peeking through the branches of the tree. Inscribed across the two stars is a quote from Romeo and Juliet: "When he shall die, take him and cut him out in little stars and he will make the face of heaven so fine that all the world will be in love with night and worship not the garish sun."

The names of each person lost in the crash are written on the back of the quilt, but in an effort to keep the special memory of Kyle's life alive forever in our hearts, we named our first child after him.

■ *During the Depression, flour and sugar sacks were used for making quilts.*

■ *In Sweden, many years ago, quilts were spread out on newly fallen snow and brushed clean using the snow.*

■ *It is believed that quilt making within Native American communities was primarily learned through contact with Euro-American culture brought by explorers, traders, and missionaries. The art was interpreted in ways that were unique to their culture. One interesting way that Native Americans used quilted fabric was to combine it with rope to create swing hammock cradles for babies.*

The E-Chat Friendship Quilt

KATHLEEN EVANOFF

Quilts have always held a special place in my heart. They represent comfort, family, and warmth. Historically, groups of women would get together in "quilting bees" to create quilts for their homes and families. Quilting bees were important for women in pioneer times. They provided the opportunity for women to connect with other women during the hard days of early American life, to create a wedding present for a local girl soon to be married, or to stitch a quilt to be sold for a charitable event. Part of the successful quilting bee experience was the relationships that developed between the women as they sat together: talking, laughing, and working toward a common goal.

Times have changed, though, and few women have the time to become involved in quilting bees. While we aren't gathering to create community around a quilting frame, we still need the intimate bonding that those experiences provided. Today many people are finding that connection virtually, through the Internet and e-mail. So what happens when a diverse group of people, spread out all over the United States, drawn together by a growing love for each other, decide to create a remembrance of the time they spent together in an Internet chat room?

Late in 1996, a group of people from all over the country who enjoyed discussing gardening, planting, and new floral varieties were attracted to a newly started chat room on the Internet. Our first conversations evolved around the quality of different varieties of compost, which plants grow best in our geographic zone, and how to acquire the newest seeds. Over time, we developed an intimacy through the depth of our written conversations.

The amazing thing about this group of friends is the fact that we didn't have the luxury of gathering around a quilt frame and looking into each other's eyes. We like to say that we learned to love each other from the "inside out," because often we felt comfortable revealing our souls through words in cyberspace when we might not have felt the same way meeting in person.

Perhaps the fact that we couldn't see each other helped to build our friendship, since we didn't always take time to think through our thoughts before sending them out in e-mails.

We came from all walks of life and we all had different life experiences, which added to the depth of our on-line conversations. Our members included nurses, photographers, professional gardeners, and homemakers. Some had children, some did not. Some are married, some aren't. We have different beliefs and moral values. The diversity added to the excitement of the group.

Over time, the group fluctuated from a high of around one hundred members to a sustained number of around forty-five participants, including men and women. As in most chat groups, mail that is sent goes out to everyone in the group as a mass mailing, so that everyone gets to see what all the others are saying. Although highly interactive, this can amount to a great deal of daily messages that have to be read and perhaps responded to. By the winter of 1998, a few of us wondered how long this friendship could last and how long we would endure the constant onslaught of e-mails. We decided that if we should someday go our separate ways, a remembrance was needed to celebrate these special friendships. That's how I got the idea for our "E-Chat Friendship Quilt." I am passionate about the heirloom value of quilts and thought this group was special enough to warrant an heirloom reminder.

Each person who chose to participate designed a six-inch fabric square. Each square proved to be an intimate snapshot of the maker in a tangible way. In designing the square, the maker was putting a bit of his or her personality on display. The color, the pattern, the fabric — each square became a reflection into the nature of the person who made it.

Nearly forty people participated, including three men. All the squares were sent to one person hosting the exchange, who in turn sorted them and sent back to each person who participated one each of all the squares created. When the squares arrived, we went to work putting them together in our own personal pattern. Some who could sew better than others in the group offered to make a few quilts, so that everyone would have one. Since our relationship is virtual, I will never see all of the other quilts, but I can reasonably say that no two would look alike. Each of us assembled our quilt in our own way.

On May 15, 1999, we lost one of our chat friends. Jeanne passed away after a long and debilitating illness. Her son very kindly wrote to us all and told us about her last days. He told us that our friendship and communication gave her strength. She constantly held her dear E-Chat quilt and it gave her comfort knowing that her friends were there with her. When I look at my quilt, with the different squares made up of different fabrics, all signed by the E-Chat members, I especially notice Jeanne's square. It is blue calico with a large seashell, outlined in puffy paint and signed "Ocean, Jeanne," just as she had signed her e-mail messages.

The group is still together and we have communicated by e-mail for more than four years now. Many of us have met face-to-face, both in large groups at organized gatherings, and in small trips to each other's homes.

Through the "E-Chat Friendship Quilt," we can hold all of our cyberfriends close and rest in the warmth created by the many hands that worked together to form this legacy. The tangible, physical presence of our virtually influenced friendship quilt helps us to take the relationships we made on-line and turn them into the real-life connections that the quilting bee participants of old experienced as they sat around the quilt frame, stitching, talking, laughing, and reflecting.

CHAPTER 5

Unexpected Surprises

*A family stitched
together with love
seldom unravels.*

Beauty Is in the Eye of the Beholder

MARCI XENIAS

The listing in the paper read, "Auction will be held Saturday, at the end of Abe Stoltzfus's farm. Look for the last farm on the left of Beiler Road, near the Stoltzfus who sold honey." Now if you knew Abe Stoltzfus, and if you knew the location of his farm, then it would be easy to attend this auction. The announcement was not printed incorrectly. It was a typical announcement for an Amish auction. If you didn't know Abe or the location of his farm, your attendance was not necessary.

My Aunt Rachel knew Abe, so I was among those fortunate ones who knew where the Stoltzfus farm was located and I was able to attend the auction that Saturday. Good food abounded, but the chicken corn soup alone was worth the trip! We bid on several items and were excited when the quilts finally came up for sale.

The Amish are a plain folk, but have a reputation for making beautiful quilts with intricate designs. The quilts being auctioned were used quilts, but were in excellent condition. An elderly Amish man sat beside me. Over his lap lay one of the finest handmade Amish quilts that I had ever seen.

The first quilt I purchased that day was a used child's embroidered block quilt in excellent condition. The next was a crazy quilt made from old wool pieces. The quilt had a few holes, but it was beautiful in my eyes. It was dated 1910 in one corner, and the initials of the quilter were in the other corner. Then came the quilt I wanted most. It was a blue-and-white block quilt with delicate embroidery. The quilt was very fragile and had a few tiny holes and snags, which I felt added to its worth. I paid five dollars for this treasure. As I sat there so excited that my heart was in my throat and I wanted to leap for joy, the Amish man sitting next to me said, "Would you like to trade seats with me as I don't think you can see what you are buying? Those are old, used quilts. You paid dear money for them. Are you sure you want them? The auctioneer may take them back for you if you ask."

He seemed so concerned for the value of my purchases that I thanked him, but told him that I really liked the quilts and would be hanging them on my walls at home. I smiled. He smiled back at me and shook his head.

I consider these quilts a treasure. The crazy quilt is mounted and displayed in my second-floor hallway. The blue-and-white quilt can be seen in my bedroom, and the child's quilt is being used by my son.

When surrounded by beauty, one can begin to take that beauty for granted. Sometimes those who have abundance lose appreciation for what they have. Sometimes one man's discarded items are another man's treasures. Beauty is truly in the eye of the beholder.

I now have memories of these quilts that will be passed on to my son and I hope his children and his children's children. The old, used quilts have taken on a new life in my home. They are loved. The handiwork of a woman, whom I will never meet, has given joy and happiness to a new family. A family that proudly displays her works of art.

An Amish quilt is not just a quilt made by Amish people, but refers to an identifiable style of quilt made by the Amish up through the early twentieth century.

Typically, Amish quilts are patchwork designs in bold geometric patterns with solid-color fabrics in distinctive colors and intricate quilting techniques. Traditionally, they were made for sons and daughters as part of their wedding dowry.

The earliest Amish quilts were very simple in their pattern and design construction. They were made of one or two colors at most. The stitching was the primary design element. Early quilts were designed in muted or natural colors with softer shades of brown, medium and darker red, gray, medium and deep blues, greens, and purples.

The motifs, colors, and designs used reflect Amish history and the group's simple outlook on life. The Amish place great value on symbolism, which enables them to create a boundary between their way of life and the outside world or the "English," as they refer to those who are not part of their church.

The Garage Sale

DONA ABBOTT

As for so many young mothers, money was a little tight. As clothing wore out at the neck, knee, and elbow, I cut swatches from the solid sections and saved them until I had enough for a quilt. I stitched them together in simple rows, with no particular artistic pattern, and backed them with red corduroy. Using blue yarn, I tied knots at regular intervals to keep the batting from shifting. This quilt was used on my son's bed for many years but remained at home when he went off to college. Although he came home for holidays, he never really lived at home again. He graduated from college, worked for a few years, and then went through graduate school to get a Ph.D. During this time, the handmade quilt rested, forgotten in a closet.

After years in the same house, my

251

storage areas were overburdened and I felt the need to do a major housecleaning to free up some new space. A garage sale seemed to be the answer. I'd just go weed through closets and get rid of a lot of things. When I came across the old quilt, so long forgotten, I had a moment of nostalgia, recalling the source of many of the materials I had used. As I examined it, heavy wear was evident in the torn seams, protruding stuffing, and the once vivid red corduroy was faded and almost smooth in places. I thought of something my sister had once said about how she keeps her closets so pristine: "If I don't use it in a year or two, I figure it's unlikely I'll ever use it again and I get rid of it." I realized that my penchant for hanging on to sentimental things had led to overflowing closets. I would just have to harden myself and get over this sentimental clinging to objects. The quilt, along with many other things, went out on the garage sale table.

A longtime friend who was browsing at the sale noticed the quilt and commented, "I can't believe you're selling this!" I went through the litany I'd chanted to convince myself to get rid of all this "stuff." A "collector" herself, she smiled understandingly.

Then she purchased the quilt to add to her own collection of "stuff."

Many years passed and finally my son settled down and began to collect things for his own apartment. "Mom," he asked me one day, "I was wondering if I could have that old quilt that used to be on my bed?" The question took me by surprise. I confessed I'd sold it at a garage sale. Now it was his turn for surprise. "Mom, how could you do that? That quilt meant so much to me! I remember the clothes that all the squares came from and I always felt so safe under it. I loved that old quilt — I just can't believe it is gone." During the years of the quilt's service, I'd never heard him say these things, but that wasn't a valid excuse. As a mother, I should have known. Now, far removed from my cleaning frenzy, I was amazed that I even thought of selling that quilt. It was totally out of character for me to do so, and now my decision was making me feel guilty and terribly sad. Worst of all, I sensed my son was disappointed in me. No wonder — I was disappointed in myself.

I called my friend to find out if she still had the quilt. Thank goodness, she did. She chuckled for a little bit. "I thought there would come a day when you might want that back," she said. There was warmth, caring, and laughter in her response. I bought it back from her, did a little mending, and gave it to my son. He's married now, but that quilt still rests lovingly on his bed, each little square imparting its own special memory of childhood.

Store quilt blocks in progress in large, clean pizza boxes from the pizza shop. Templates can also be stored in this same box.

Store completed quilts rolled with old sheets, blankets, towels, or 100 percent cotton mattress pads in them to prevent creases from folds. Lay them on a long shelf.

Avoid exposing quilts directly to untreated wood, such as a cedar chest or closet shelves. Place them in a large pillowcase or wrap with a sheet.

■ ■ ■

Significant in the Life of a Child

LIZ WADE

I was not prepared for what I was about to see, but it changed my perspective on quilting forever. The event only lasted fifteen seconds, but it indelibly remains in my memory.

As was our habit, the family videos came out and were played while my husband and I visited his sister and brother-in-law. These videos allowed each of us to share the growth of our grandchildren with the other. They put their video in the player and quietly let me watch as their two-year-old grandson toddled into the backyard where his mother had hung the laundry. There in the middle of the line was the baby quilt I had made for him when he was born. Suddenly he dropped his toy, ran over to the laundry line, stuck his thumb in his mouth, reached to grab the corner of his quilt, and proceeded to rub it against his cheek — despite the fact that it was soaking wet. At that moment, I knew why I was a quilter.

Perhaps I became "misty" because this sight was so unexpected, so spontaneous, and so unsolicited. Many children have a special item that makes them feel secure. For some, it is their thumb. For others, it is a special blanket. In this case, the special item was a quilt — one that I had made.

It came as a total surprise. I had been told that he loved the quilt, but had no idea how much. In the past, I have made quilts for the pleasure of designing and executing that design. But suddenly, when I saw this small child's unrehearsed display of endearment, it was evident to me that there was so much more enjoyment to quilting than that which is received from designing and finishing a quilt. If I gave a quilt as a gift, I knew that it would be appreciated but not necessarily loved. When that love was shown, the reward was unexpected, amazing, and beyond any kind of thankfulness that I could ever anticipate.

■ *Always cut the largest pieces of fabric first. The leftover scraps can be used for the smaller pieces.*

■ *Flea markets, yard sales, and garage and estate sales are great places to buy bargain fabrics or garments that can be washed and cut up for quilt fabric.*

The Mystery of the Missing Sunbonnet Sue

PHYLLIS J. KOSHEWITZ

A few years ago, Karen, a fellow member of my Sunday school class, announced that she was going to begin teaching a quilting class. I had put my sewing skills in hibernation as my two children grew up. In addition, teaching full-time siphoned away extra energy for close work like stitching. However, upon hearing about the quilting class, my curiosity was sparked.

All I knew about quilting was that my step grandmother, Goldie, had made me a quilt when I was a young girl. I began to appreciate it when I reached my forties. Viewing Goldie's quilt gave me renewed inspiration, and I called to sign up for the class.

Six or eight ladies arrived for the first class. It took several trips to the car to carry in all the paraphernalia and lay it on the three or four tables stretched end to end. There were many different brands of sewing machines and many new gadgets. They brought in plastic cutting boards with grid lines, rotary cutters (which looked like sharp pizza cutters to me), a great variety of rainbow-colored "Gutermann" thread (never heard of it before), and "Gingher" (who?) scissors. The women had quilting safety pins that were bent (on purpose), wooden crayons called markers (my markers were scented and had felt tips), irons, extension cords, and the tiniest needles I had ever seen. They exhibited quite an air of expertise. So not to look like the complete novice that I was, I watched quietly and tried to copy what they did. Thus, we began creating a quilt.

Over the weeks, we carefully learned to cut fabric, fold it, and piece it. As the class progressed, we became friends and enjoyed adult chitchat. We had fun assisting each other as the classes continued. Karen told us about entering different quilting contests. I sat ripping out bad stitches, feeling as though a contest had to be at least a hundred years away for me! She told us that judges are so concerned with the quality of the work that they hold the quilts that they are judging up to the light to see if the seam widths inside are correct. Sometimes they even look inside for stray, unclipped threads! *Wow!* I worked neatly and carefully, but these stories made me feel overwhelmed and sometimes discouraged! Nevertheless, with the encouragement of the others, I kept at it. Besides, as a teacher working with children all day, the adult conversation was enjoyable.

I kept my family informed about my snail-like quilting progress. My father teasingly said, "I can't for the life of me figure out why a perfectly normal person like you would take a perfectly good piece of fabric, cut it all apart, and then sew the pieces back together again!" It just didn't make sense to him. I tried to explain the precision needed in cutting, the care needed in sewing, the need for coordinating fabrics, and the geometry involved in the process, but it had absolutely no impact on him. My mother, however, who quilted as a child, was, I think, rather pleased that I was developing such an interest. She showed me the quilts that she had collected over the years and told me who made them — her mother, her stepmother, or herself, and told the stories of their origin. To me, all the quilts seemed to end up in one of two categories: saved in the cedar chest or completely worn out.

One that became worn out was my favorite childhood "Sunbonnet Sue" quilt. I recalled sitting on my bed, pretending that the feed sack "Sues" were my dolls. They were dressed to go to church — or wherever my imagination took them. Over the years of hard use, Sue's cheerful, dated feed sack outfits had faded. Mother, who saved everything, sewed blocks of fabric together to form a duvet cover (of sorts) for the worn-out quilt, knotted the cover in place, and then sewed the edges shut. After the cover was sewn shut, the likeness of the old tattered quilt was out of sight and out of mind (quickly forgotten). She covered many of the quilts at our home because a family of seven required a lot of bedding and the newly covered quilts lasted many more years. In fact, we grew up and started carrying our quilts to our own homes. As grandchildren came along and grew up, they got some of Grandma's quilts. Others were sold at garage sales. Some simply became too worn to salvage and were finally discarded.

Karen's class prompted me to think of my childhood "Sunbonnet Sue" quilt. I not only started to think about it, I began to obsess about it! I yearned to see my "Sunbonnet Sue" quilt again. For whatever reason, I just wanted to reach back into my childhood and relish the wondrous imaginative hours of play that I had enjoyed as a little girl. As the class progressed, I thought more and more about my old quilt.

I asked Mother where Sue was. Of course, she had no idea. She remembered that Sue had seen her better days and had been covered years ago. Besides, nearly all of Mother's covered quilts were scattered within the family. I did not want to hear this explanation! However, I bit my lower lip and with heaviness in my heart, knew that I would never see my quilt again. I felt disappointment for days after this realization.

My hectic work schedule and the approaching Christmas holidays demanded that I forget my preoccupation for the lost quilt and begin preparing for a weeklong visit from our daughter. It seemed that her visit came and went much too quickly.

Still full of the moments we shared together, I began clearing her bedding for laundering. Gathering it together, it occurred to me that one of Mother's covered quilts was among the bedding. On a whim, I dropped everything else and looked lovingly at the leftover factory patches that

Mother had sewn together so long ago. I stretched the blanket across the bare mattress, ran my fingers along the seams, and noticed that there was barely a ripped thread anywhere. The knots were just as intact as the day she tied them. The pattern on the material was understandably faded from years of use in my home, but the blanket was cozy and was always used on a bed somewhere.

On impulse, I picked up a corner and, as we had been taught in my quilting class, held it up to the sunlight that was streaming in through the double windows behind the bed. I heard a catch in my own breath, and my eyes widened — then widened some more as I peered through the blanket into the sunlight. I looked closer and yet closer. My heartbeat increased. Tears started to fill my eyes. I felt a lump in my throat as I hugged the blanket and raced to the next room to grab my seam ripper. I began to rip stitches from the bound edges quickly but carefully. I grabbed the telephone and dialed my mother. "Mother, you'll never guess what I'm doing! I have found her! She has been in my own house all these years! What are the chances that I would ever find her? I've found my Sunbonnet Sue!"

Group activities are an important part of the Amish lifestyle.

Amish women often get together for major housecleaning, moving preparations, and sewing projects.

When an Amish woman finishes a quilt top she invites about twelve people for a quilting party. The guests may be a group composed of her sisters and cousins, or the party can extend to include neighbors and other family members.

The quilters sit around the four sides of the frame and work from the outer edges toward the center. When the women seated along the top and bottom have quilted as far as they can reach, the quilt is rolled, decreasing the work space along the sides of the frame, requiring fewer hands.

It usually takes more than a day but less than two days to finish the quilt. Women arrive around nine o'clock in the morning and stay until about four o'clock in the afternoon, eating dinner served by the hostess at noon.

■ ■ ■

The Littlest Granddaughter

MALINDA K. OAKES

My grandmother seemed old to me, somewhere in her eighties, I guess. Every time we went to visit her, she was in the same place, sitting in her overstuffed living room chair, working on a puzzle. She wore old ladies' dresses that she made herself, stockings that she rolled to below her knees, and black lace-up shoes. Her glasses were thick because of cataracts and made her eyes look big and a little strange to me. But when she was tickled about something, the sparkle that twinkled in those eyes looked like light reflecting from a diamond. Her chuckle could fill a room with cheer.

I looked forward to our family's biweekly visits with her, which required me to always be on my best behavior, but this visit was extraspecial. Grandma had called the whole family together. All my cousins would be there. It was the day she had chosen to allow the grandchildren to choose one of her quilts to be their very own.

Grandma, following the tradition of birthright, allowed us to go up the divided staircase to her bedroom one at a time — the oldest grandchild first, the youngest grandchild last. This was a great arrangement if you happened to be the oldest grandchild, but I was the youngest of eight!

With each cousin who came back down those stairs, arms laden with one of Grandma's beautiful quilts, I became more anxious. The more anxious I became, the more fidgety I grew. The wait for my turn seemed like an eternity.

"Which one did you pick?" I would ask as each grandchild took his or her place back in the living room. The quilts were all so beautiful to me but my fear mounted as I wondered what would be left for me.

Finally! My turn! I hurried up to select my quilt. It was easy. It was the only one left! It felt so heavy and I was so small. I called to Mom for help and she opened it up for me when we got downstairs.

It wasn't nearly as large as it felt.

"Grandma, is it big enough to fit my bed?" I inquired. She chuckled as she replied with a twinkle, "It's big enough to keep you warm."

It had such a pretty, bright turquoise border. Really, it was the most colorful of any of the others. Mom began to point out different fabrics to me. Many were from her own sewing projects.

The colors were attractive. I was so happy that this was the quilt that was left, but since I thought it was the prettiest of all, I wondered why none of the others had chosen it. Perhaps it was because of its size. I loved the quilt as I took it home with me, but I didn't know at that time the treasure that laid waiting for discovery in this "cover" that my birth order had afforded me.

Years later, when I could understand the importance, I found out that it was the last quilt Grandma ever made. Had I received one of the other quilts, I would have been glad to have it, but there is no way that any other quilt could have had the significance to me that this one did. The others were made before I could remember. Their materials were carefully matched and their patterns beautifully executed. The fabrics in my quilt were a hodgepodge of scraps haphazardly gathered just for something to pass the time. But that's not how I saw it. Therein laid the treasure!

Now as I look at the kaleidoscope of colors, I not only see my grandmother, but also a dress my mother wore, Dad's PJs, and matching outfits that my mother made for my sister and me. My childhood is in that quilt, preserved forever, just waiting for me to come and reminisce. No other treasure could be greater.

Some quilters avoid using polyester fabrics because they are slippery to work with. To test a fabric that is not marked, rub a double layer of fabric between your fingers. If it's 100 percent polyester, it will slide easily between your fingers. It also has a sheen and will reflect the light.

Fabrics that are a combination of polyester and cotton will catch slightly; 100 percent cotton will grip the other layer when rubbed together.

Fabrics can also be given a fold test, which is simply folding the fabric and running your nail along the fold. Fabrics that are 100 percent cotton hold a crease. Polyester and poly/cotton blends do not crease well.

Do a burn test if you are unsure of fabric content. Burn a scrap; if the residue is soft and gray, the fabric is cotton. The fabric is a blend if the burn test produces a hard-beaded residue.

■ ■ ■

Stitches in Time

KAREN B. ALEXANDER

How do I remember Wini? Let me count the ways — or better yet, let me recount the stitches! Oh my, the stitches! This seemingly tireless woman gave so much of herself through both her teaching and her creations, and truly allowed love to flow through the creations she made for her children and grandchildren.

I am a quilt historian and passionately study fabric and stitching. That's why my mother-in-law, Wini, was so fascinating to me. In retrospect, it is obvious how many of our family memories revolve around her stitched creations, there were so many: the stuffed toys, the needlepoint Christmas stockings, and the quilts!

My favorite memories were Wini's quilts. First she made the quilts that the children used during childhood. Then she created quilts from jeans, with a built-in tote bag pieced into the center that accompanied the children to college. The quilts that eventually graced their marriage beds came next and then the baby quilts for the great-grandchildren that soon followed. Our lives were filled with Wini's quilts.

Her life was paradoxical in many ways. Wini was an intelligent, well-versed, and highly educated woman who taught others the art of caring for family and home but experienced great personal insecurity about her own abilities. Even though she often lacked an awareness of her own self-worth, she was continually building the self-worth of others.

Born Winifred Margaret Waters in Yakima, Washington, Wini lost her mother to tuberculosis when she was only six years old. Her childhood was thereafter an endless series of homes, schools, stepmothers, and caregivers. Her restless, authoritarian father sought to make sense of his changed world and consequently, Wini attended sixteen different schools in eight years. The scars of the loss of her mother, varying caregivers, and constant moves left a deep and painful sense of insecurity and ongoing need for acknowledgment in Wini.

Yet her own indomitable spirit and her love of needlework, especially quilting, would prove to be her saving grace throughout her life. In her older years, quilting became her journey to self-esteem.

We greatly enhance our children's self-esteem when we acknowledge and honor their creative endeavors. I have often wondered if Wini consciously understood how deeply she affirmed her grandchildren. When our oldest daughter, Sarah, entered kindergarten, we began sending her school artwork to Wini. To our delight, unbeknownst to us, Wini collected these treasures and translated each into needlework. After she collected enough art, she composed an incredible, prizewinning quilt from the translated works of art and gave it to Sarah. It will be a lasting reminder of her grandmother's tremendous love for her.

The same year, Sarah came home from school with a full-length body portrait of herself, traced onto brown butcher paper. This was done to help each child see his or her uniqueness, consequently building self-esteem. Our two younger children immediately clamored to make one too. Soon, with help, the outline of two more little bodies appeared on paper. Each child then excitedly drew his or her own features and clothes.

By this time, the children had grown to love sending their artwork to Grandma, knowing that she appreciated it. All three eagerly wanted to send their portraits for Grandma to see. Little did they know that they were in for a big surprise come Christmas! Three life-size portrait quilts were under the Christmas tree!

I often photographed my children holding their gifts of stitchery from Wini. To this day, my favorite photo of her needlework was taken the very first Christmas she and Grandpa were able to join us for the holidays. The photo shows the children tucked into camping cots covered by their full-body portrait quilts that Grandma had just given them that morning. Their faces were wreathed in huge grins. To make the portrait quilts even more individual and special, building appreciation for their uniqueness, each appliquéd figure was clothed in remnants of fabric matching clothes that Wini had previously made for the children to wear.

I remember how proudly the children wore the clothes she made for them. To this day, several special outfits are tucked safely away for future generations to view and appreciate. Not only did Wini make the children feel special, but she also preserved our past by showing a figure of the children at that age, dressed in material from their own clothes.

In February 1999, Wini was diagnosed with terminal ovarian cancer. The quilting guild to which she belonged made a "comfort quilt" of many hearts signed by her friends. She kept it at the foot of the hospice bed in which she lay and proudly showed it to all her visitors.

The evening she passed on, we spread the quilt over her for the night. Since she was cremated, we were unable to drape the quilt over or place it in a casket; however, at her memorial service, we hung several of her quilts, including this special "comfort quilt." We had other mementos laid out on tables around the room, such as her quilted clothing; the last small hexagon piece she worked on while confined to bed; the basket in which she kept quilt pieces and sewing tools; a small photo album filled with her favorite quilts as well as photos of the grandchildren with the quilts she had made them; and a memory book of her life.

As a result of her bequeathing to me her quilt studio and everything in it, I discovered an unexpected treasure — a few journals from her earliest years. In one of those journals she wrote of her first attempts at quilting in 1945, just months before her only son, my future husband, was born. I treasured the peek into the past. She could not have known how much future generations would treasure the results of her efforts when she experienced self-doubt in her earlier quilting days.

In a journal entry dated January 17, 1945, she writes: "I started cutting quilt patches out of rose muslin and assorted scraps. Wonder how it will look?" (Elsewhere in her journal, she writes that these scraps were old and used curtains that she dyed and tried to make into quilt fabric.) Years later, Wini jotted a short note in a journal that she was never much of a success at "this first quilting attempt." The quilt became a floor covering in the baby's playroom and later a cover for furniture moving.

Without knowing it, perhaps the focus that she placed upon meeting others' needs distracted Wini from her own inadequacies, ironically allowing her own self-confidence to silently build. Upon going through files after her death, I discovered a priceless jewel that comforted me. It was a draft of a story written by Wini, a woman who in spite of her self-doubt had found such joy and self-confidence through quilting and needlework that she was able to write a major women's magazine telling the story of Sarah's quilt.

I also learned that Sarah's artwork gave Wini the inspiration she had been seeking for teaching new quilting methods in her sewing class! "You reap what you sew" surely rang true in Wini's life. She stitched love, honor, and self-esteem into the lives of others and reaped the same abundantly by the end of her life. Her story is captured within the stitched journals of her life for future generations and as we sleep under them, we continue to savor her memory.

■ *When shopping for fabric, take a needle along with you and practice a few quilting stitches, minus the thread, on the fabric to see how easily the needle flows through the fabric.*

■ *When marking fabrics, a silver or yellow pencil shows up on both dark and light fabrics. Soap slivers or small travel soaps are great on medium or dark fabrics. Use a dotted line rather than a solid line — the fabric is less likely to move and there is less marking to re-move later.*

The Postcard "Name" Quilt

EMMA BEVACQUA

I was first introduced to quilting when I was nine years old.

My family was well known in our little community along the banks of the Ohio River in rural Kentucky, since my father owned a country grocery store. Even though it was during the Depression, it was not as hard for us as for some others thanks to the revenue generated by the store. My mother belonged to the Ladies Aid Society, a very active group that held ice cream socials, bake sales, craft sales — anything to raise money for the church.

It was fund-raising time again — the church needed hymnals and Sunday school leaflets. So the Ladies Aid Society commissioned a quilt to be made and sold at auction.

The hullabaloo of preparation was exciting. It was the first year that I was allowed to participate because I had learned how to embroider. I was given the job of soliciting people who wanted their names forever embroidered onto a quilt square. For this particular quilt, squares were made the size of postcards and had a design embroidered in the upper right-hand corner that looked like a stamp. For ten cents, one could have his name and address embroidered on the white cotton square with bright red floss in the "address" field.

Traditionally, when enough squares were sold, they were stitched together into a quilt top, quilted, and then sold at auction. But for some reason this top was never quilted or brought to auction. It ended up in my mother's cedar chest for safekeeping and eventually, my father donated the money to cover the customary price a typical quilt would have brought at auction.

After high school, I went away to college, married, and eventually moved to North Carolina. My father died and my mother went to live with my younger sister in Pittsburgh, Pennsylvania.

On one of my visits with my mother, my sister and I started rummaging through my mother's cedar chest and found that old quilt top. We talked and giggled as we reminisced about the people whose names were embroidered. We were able to recall faces with some of the names that we saw. There was the man who liked snakes — we didn't like to be around him; the man who sold blackberries and peddled them; the blind man who tuned pianos! It was amazing that after all the years that had gone by, we were still able to clearly remember whom we liked and whom we did not like. Our little Kentucky community still lived!

Reliving the past through our memories made me want to quilt the top for my mother. So my sister helped me sneak it out of her house and I took it back to North Carolina, quilted it, and then sent it back to my mother on Mother's Day.

Being quiet in nature, Mother never said too much about anything, so I was very pleased when she wrote a sweet note to me after receiving the quilt. She was amazed and wondered when I ever had the time to finish it.

The foot of her bed became the quilt's home and often, when I visited, Mother would spread the quilt out over the whole bed. Along with my sister, the three of us recalled our old home place.

My Uncle Jim paid ten cents to have his name on the quilt and when I saw his name, I remembered how he used to grow peonies. From the time I was four or five years old until I went away to college, Uncle Jim always saved the first peony blossom for me and always found a way to deliver it to me, even though we lived several miles apart.

When I saw the mailman's name, I remembered that he stopped at Uncle Jim's house first, and then eventually got to my house. Then I remembered that Uncle Jim often sent the peony blossom with Corbit, the mailman.

Corbit was a chunky little man with a chuckle for a laugh and carried the mail for as long as I can remember. Because of his shape and the way he laughed, he always reminded me of Santa Claus.

One memory led to another. Slowly my childhood in our little town didn't seem so long ago. Mother pointed out my Aunt Effie's name on the quilt. Pleasant memories of my father came to me as I thought about how he allowed me to go with him when he made his rounds to get grocery orders. It was particularly exciting to me to go with him because it meant that I could go to Aunt Effie's house and read the color "funny pages" from the newspaper — a real treat!

Mother passed away and now the "Postcard 'Name' Quilt" resides at the foot of my bed. I have five granddaughters who now "ooh" and "aah" while opening the quilt. The years fall away for me when I hear them giggle as I tell them the stories of the man who drove the truck, and the man who owned a mule but always beat it, and the man who drove the tractor that ran away, and my uncle. I worked for him for fifty cents a day dropping tobacco plants. I told how I would walk in front of the planter, drop the tobacco plants, and then the planter would come behind me to put the plant in the ground. We didn't even get lunch!

It made me happy when one of my granddaughters made me promise to leave the quilt to her. She will continue to tell the stories in the "Name Quilt" of my little community, and the legacy will live on.

Quilt Tips:

■ *Don't shop for fabric if you are in a bad mood or not feeling well. It may affect the colors you choose.*

■ *Don't quilt under stress. You may have to remove the section you finished the next day because the stitches are too tight.*

■ *Don't eat chocolate when you are quilting.*

■ *Background music or a pleasant view help to make a comfortable quilting atmosphere.*

■ *Record the progress of your quilt project in a journal, recording your daily work. Record design problems, progress, feelings about a piece, changes, batting type, machine settings, techniques, even what is going on in the news that day, and the amount of time spent each day the quilt is worked on.*

■ *Don't do dishes or participate in water sports before quilting; it softens the skin.*

My Quilting Lesson

DEB HOPKINS

For years my cedar chest has held a myriad of things, but there is a strict criterion for admission. To be included in this elite membership, it must be a treasure — at least in my eyes.

Recently I pulled two quilt tops from the corner of my cedar chest where they had been lovingly tucked away for a number of years. The memories that these quilt tops stirred filled my heart with emotions. My closest friend, Wanda, entrusted them to me. She wanted me to finish the quilts for her sons.

If cloth could talk, what a tale these threads would spin! The tale begins with an old humpbacked chest. This chest, with the domed lid designed to safely pack hats, belonged to Wanda's grandmother and was part of their belongings on the big move cross-country.

In the 1920s, Wanda's grandmother and entire family traveled from Illinois to Wyoming. They weren't able to bring their belongings with them, so they had to be shipped ahead of them via cargo rail cars.

Travel was hard and slow for the family, especially for Wanda's mother, being seven months pregnant. It took ten days just to travel from St. Louis to Wyoming. They traveled across the country in three or four touring cars — cumbersome, open-air cars specifically made very large so an entire family unit could travel together. Even though pregnant, Wanda's mother and her family had to sleep on the ground next to the trail, just like the other travelers.

They followed little more than a cow path called the "Yellow Stone Road" to the west that was marked only by stones painted yellow to help keep them headed in the right direction. The family settled in Powell, Wyoming, which is just sixty miles away from what is now known as Yellowstone National Park.

When it arrived, the old humpbacked chest was stored. It was passed from Wanda's grandmother to Wanda's mother. As years went by the chest was covered by other items that slowly accumulated, burying it and causing it to be forgotten.

Years later, after the death of her parents and while she was organizing their estate, Wanda uncovered the old chest in her parents' storage building. Curiously opening the chest, she found the quilt tops that she later entrusted to my care.

Knowing that I owned a long-arm sewing machine designed for stitching quilts, Wanda asked if I would quilt the two tops. One top, "Grandmother's Flower Garden," had been exquisitely pieced together entirely by hand, and was without a doubt the best handiwork I've ever seen.

My heart ached at the thought of touching this beautiful top with my machine. Being a true-to-the-core quilter, I could not imagine finishing "Grandmother's Flower Garden," having such a high caliber of hand stitching, by machine — to me it would be a sin.

I explained to Wanda that the value of the quilts would be much greater if they were hand quilted and referred her to very good hand quilters. Respecting my opinion, she met with the hand quilters, but found that the cost was prohibitive. To Wanda, the importance did not lie in the method of stitching, but in her desire to see the quilts passed on to her sons, preserving heritage.

She returned to persuade me to quilt the tops by machine. I think I felt much more stress about this endeavor than Wanda did. I knew that she didn't have many keepsakes from her family. These tops were her prized possessions. It was much easier for me to set the tops aside and dismiss the task than to touch them with my machine — thus they came to rest in my chest. It took years for me to build enough courage to do the quilting. Wanda waited patiently.

I always admired the art of quilting, so I periodically brought "Grandmother's Flower Garden" out of my chest to study the stitching and the use of the pink and green colors. One day, several years after Wanda gave the tops to me, I pulled the cherished "Grandmother's Flower Garden" top out of my chest and decided to start quilting it.

I carefully selected white-on-white fabric for the backing and stretched the quilt over my machine. My heart began to pound with apprehension as I loaded all my bobbins with white thread and then carefully checked my machine one final time to ensure that all was perfect. I was now ready to begin quilting. I took a slow, deep breath as I put the needle down, and pulled up the first thread. With a simple touch of a button, I committed myself to completing this quilt by machine.

Row by row, the quilting took shape. Sometimes I would bite my tongue and hold my breath as I eased the needle and thread through the older bits of fabric. I was so careful to hold it tight and stitch through every hexagon piece. With a flourish, the final few stitches completed this step of the process. The quilt was almost finished. I felt my body begin to relax as I carefully removed it from the frame. As I draped it over my arm and carried it away to be trimmed, I felt like the maker of the quilt was telling me, in her own way, that what I had done was right.

When all the work was completed, I called Wanda. I have since forgotten her exact words, but my heart will never forget the sound of tears in her voice as she thanked me. Little did she know that the quilt had already spoken to my heart.

I sent the finished quilt to her and received a long letter in response. The words on the page came to life when she told of running her hands over the quilt and feeling the warmth and love held within the many tiny stitches made so many years ago. While reading Wanda's words of thanks, I felt as if the maker put her arms around me in a big hug, also thanking me. At long last, I knew all was well. This quilt, found in an old humpbacked trunk so long ago, had come full circle. Not only will it be treasured and used within the family as it was meant to be, but it also taught me a valuable lesson. Quilts have been an expression of love through the ages. The maker puts heart and soul into every stitch, knowing that her love will be felt through the warmth that the quilt provides through the ages. The importance lies, not in the method of stitching, but in the expression. I could feel it in my heart. An overwhelming sense of peace, contentment, and love fills my soul when I think of it.

Desert warriors of the southern Sahara used quilting and patchwork to create horse armor. The riders also wore quilted armor, but not as intricately designed as that of their horses. The armor protected the horses against arrows and other weapons.

Hand-woven and hand-colored cotton cloth was cut and sewn into traditional patchwork designs like "Flying Geese" and "Windmill."

The patchwork fabric was cut into shapes that fit over the saddle — almost hanging to the horse's feet, a neck wrap to cover the horse's chest, and a shield for the horse's head.

Horse armor can be seen today, worn by military companies turning out in ceremonial processions and parades.

■ ■ ■

The Secret Garden

LIZ BERNSTEIN

For Lindsay Kay, my four-year-old and youngest daughter, it was hard to "sit like a lady" when visiting her grandparents. It took a long car ride from Ohio to get to their New York home and Lindsay found it hard to contain herself after sitting so long on the journey.

Seeing Lindsay's need to release some energy after the trip, her grandma would wisely send her on "missions" to the third-floor attic. Lindsay, being of a curious nature, took advantage of the situation and turned the missions into "exploration expeditions."

Following the new tradition that had been formed, this particular trip was no different from the others *until* Lindsay discovered pay dirt on her expedition! Running down the stairs in excitement and holding her treasure in her hands, Lindsay exclaimed, "Look, Grandma, I finded flowers in your attic!"

Upon closer examination of her findings, her grandma and I discovered that Lindsay was holding white, pink, and green shapes in her little hands. There in her tiny hands, Lindsay held the most beautiful bouquet of flowers in the guise of partially completed quilt blocks! She had indeed found flowers in the attic, but unbeknownst to Lindsay, the treasure that she had found held far greater worth than she knew.

Lindsay had found a box that several years earlier had been brought to Grandma's house when her mother's house was "broken up" following her death. Grandma had never examined the contents of the box; it was just placed in the attic. Lindsay's grandmother was thrilled with the discovery. The find was especially valuable because she had recently become interested in quilting and its history. She couldn't put a name to the pattern, although it very closely resembled several other well-known quilt patterns. Grandma determined that the quilt had probably been started by her Aunt Mae Purdie Wade, an elegant woman who lived, until her death in the 1920s, in an affluent part of Westchester County.

Most women in that day only had time and money enough to make quilts to keep the family warm, but Aunt Mae was one of the few members of this family who could afford to sew out of love for art and beauty. These newly discovered quilt blocks were far more intricate than most quilts made in that era.

Searching long and hard to match the faded seventy-year-old fabric, Grandma and Grandpa spent the rest of the winter completing the quilt by hand. Without a guide or pattern, they turned the odd shapes and almost finished blocks into a wonderful work of art. Lacking a formal pattern, Grandpa suggested that Grandma quilt the blocks, using the outline of the appliquéd pattern. He traced it for her, and she carefully hand stitched each block.

When good weather for traveling finally arrived, Grandpa and Grandma made a trip to our Ohio home. Proudly, they presented a lovely, wrapped package to Lindsay. With excitement, Lindsay opened the package to find her treasured flowers stitched into "her quilt."

Hearing our exclamations, Lindsay solemnly announced that I could have the use of her quilt until she "got big" and had her own house. Since then, her quilt has hung, first in Ohio and now in New York, as a centerpiece in our home. However, lest I become too attached and forget, a now sixteen-year-old Lindsay reminds me that her treasure is merely on loan.

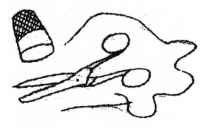

Contributors[*]

DONA ABBOTT is an artist living in Boulder, Colorado. She can be contacted through her Web site at http://members.aol.com/dabbott303.

KAREN B. ALEXANDER has been a member of the American Quilt Study Group since 1981, and is currently a board member of the Quilter's Hall of Fame, which is located in Marion, Indiana. She also writes her own genealogy newsletter and occasional quilt history–related articles. Karen may be contacted at Folkquilt@aol.com.

ANNA H. BEDFORD served as director of communications for Heifer Project International, an organization that helps hungry people worldwide with gifts of livestock and training. She has also served as editor of

*Please refer to page 309 for explanations of contributors' designations.

Horizons, a global women's issues magazine. A native of Cardiff, Wales, she has also lived in Yunnan, China, and Nairobi, Kenya. She now resides in Little Rock, Arkansas.

PATT BELL, CCD, CPD, is a professional craft designer. She has been married to Jack, her best friend, for thirty-eight years. They have four children and four grandchildren. Patt can be contacted at pattbell@aol.com.

PENNY BERENS of Ontario, Canada, is a fiber artist whose award-winning quilts incorporate texture and embroidery. As a teacher, she encourages creativity and self-expression. Penny can be contacted at berens@home.com.

LIZ BERNSTEIN is a wife, mother of three, and mother-in-law of two. She lives in western New York. She enjoys sharing family stories.

EMMA BEVACQUA lives in Raleigh, North Carolina, with her husband. She has nine grandchildren. Emma is a retired high school biology teacher of thirty years. She enjoys quilting and stitching costumes for local theaters.

BRENDA BULLOCK lives in central Arkansas

with Howard, her best friend and husband of thirty-five years. They have three adult children and two grandchildren. When she has spare time, she saves it for antiquing and needle art.

ISABELLE CARLSON is a certified public accountant living in Modesto, California. She has been blessed with sixteen grandchildren.

MARY COLLINS is a registered nurse by profession, but these days spends all her time caring for her two children — Kyle, age three, and Mary Grace, age two. She and her husband, John, reside in a quiet rural town where she spends free time sewing and quilting. Mary is a member of the "Crazy Quilter's Quilt Guild" in Allentown, Pennsylvania.

MARGARET B. COOLICAN, RN, M.S., CDE, has been active in public and professional education in the areas of bereavement and organ and tissue donation since 1985. A certified death educator, she is founding editor of the national newsletter *For Those Who Grieve*, written for donor families, and is the founding and immediate past chair of the National Donor Family Council (NDFC), a national organization of donor families. Ms. Coolican has spoken throughout the country and published extensively in the areas of organ and tissue donation and the care of families in crisis. Her greatest joy is as a wife and mother of six children. She can be contacted at coolicanm@aol.com.

BRENDA DIAL is a wife and mother of three, with one child in the navy. She works with computers and is currently the manager of information services in Hopkins County, Texas. With a full-time job and full-time family, she feels quilting and writing keep her sane. She has been quilting for twenty-six years.

KATHLEEN EVANOFF is a married mother of two grown children, a master gardener, and a news correspondent for a local newspaper.

SARA FELTON is the director of marketing and sales for the Great American Quilt Factory quilt shop and Possibilities books in Denver, Colorado. The "Love Letters" quilt can be found in the Possibilities book *Hearts Aplenty.* For more information on creating your own healing quilt, please contact her at info@greatamericanquilt.com.

CAROLINA FERNANDEZ, M.B.A., relies heavily on her brood of four to gain inspiration for a boutique line of children's playwear. They also provide great material for writing and public speaking. Fourteen years of motherhood enabled her to write *Planet Motherhood*, her first book. She enjoys blissful chaos in Miami, Florida, with her husband, Ernie, and children, Nicolas, Benjamin, Cristina, and Victor; Doodlebug, the guinea pig; and Isabella, the Bichon Frise. Contact her at 305-256-9088 or emomrx@yahoo.com.

BILL GARDNER is a trade magazine editor and has been active in AIDS fund-raising for several years. He is cofounder of "Creating for Life," an auction of handcrafted items, including quilts, that has raised more than a quarter of a million dollars for AIDS research, education, and services.

MIKE HARTNETT is a magazine columnist and publisher of *Creative Leisure News*, a trade newsletter for the arts and crafts industry. Contact him at mhartnet@ix.netcom. com. Visit his Web site at www.clnonline.com.

RALPH HOOD, CSP, is a funny man, according to Oprah. He is a full-time professional speaker and writer whose travels have taken him to all fifty states plus Canada. He is author of The Truth & Other Lies and writes for several national trade publications. Contact him at 800-828-3802 or hoodspeak@cs.com.

DEB HOPKINS is married to a retired Canadian military officer. She has been quilting for more than twenty years, and has designed many quilting patterns. She was the codesigner of the "Wonder Cut Ruler." Contact her at quiltie@pmt.org. A gallery of her work can be seen at www.wondercutruler.com.

LIBBY KACZYNSKI is a widow living in Florida. She and her husband, Len, raised four children. She is now enjoying her seven grandchildren and three great-grandchildren. A strong family bond continues among them all.

PHYLLIS J. KOSHEWITZ is a seasoned, award-winning public school teacher in Pennsylvania. She and her husband are the parents of two adult children.

PATRICIA LADERER is a sometime writer, artist, gardener, and "Nana" to grandson Cole. She has been blessed with a wonderful marriage to Presbyterian minister John Laderer. You may contact her at presbyrev@juno.com.

JOE LAMANCUSA JR. is an explorer. A

summa cum laude graduate of Miami University in Oxford, Ohio, his major prepared him for a life as a manager in corporate America. However, he sees himself maybe teaching English in Nepal, or studying rain forests in Australia, or perhaps being a college professor so he can inspire passion in his students. Joe feels the only things in life one regrets are the risks one doesn't take. He is the author of *Kid Cash: Creative Money-Making Ideas*, published by McGraw-Hill.

DEBBI LIEBERSON is a writer living in Cambridge, Massachusetts, with her son, Ben. She is currently working on a memoir that explores the complex and unconventional friendship she shared with an HIV-positive man and his relationship with her young son. "The Heart of the Matter," which appears in this work, was previously published in December 1999 in *The Boston Globe Magazine*. Debbi Lieberson can be contacted at dblieberso@aol.com or 617-661-1810.

MARY MAYFIELD is a retired teacher. Her husband and children call her a professional volunteer. She enjoys travel, taking classes, and creating new programs and workshops for church, school, clubs, and quilting groups. However, being a grandmother is her favorite job. She lives in Nebraska, where quilting has always been a cherished activity.

SARAH JANE MCMILLEN is currently living in Miami, Florida, with her husband, Bert, and their German shepherd, Sage. She is actively involved in painting with watercolor, quilting, and stained-glass design.

ELAINE MEYLAN is a lifelong student. As a child, she learned about her family history from her paternal grandmother. As a mother, she believes she has learned as much about life from her three grown children as they have from her. As a substitute teacher, she learns daily in a variety of classrooms. As a wife, she discovers the value of commitment in her twenty-eight-year marriage. She resides in Colorado, where she enjoys a variety of domestic arts, horseback riding, and hiking.

SIMONE MORTAN is a science educator at the Monterey Bay Aquarium. Her creative interests include storytelling, fiber arts, spinning, and weaving. She is currently learning about quilting by piecing a quilt of hand-woven overshot squares.

MALINDA K. OAKES, her husband, Galen, daughter, Joy, and son, Nolan, work as a ministry team in an effort to strengthen relationships within the family unit. Using original drama, music, costumes, and group participation activities, they bring themed adventures to audiences in church and camp settings. As third-generation homebuilders, Galen and Malinda enjoy helping others build their "dream home" in both a physical and a spiritual sense. For more information, contact them at GalenAndMalinda@aol.com.

JOSEPHINE MCCLOUD ORETO is a seventy-four-year-old widowed mother of six children. She lost one son when he was fifteen and a second son in the Vietnam War when he was twenty-one. She was formerly active in church and community affairs and now fills her hours with gardening, canning, quilting, and other hobbies. She cares for her 105-year-old mother, loves living in a small town, and her favorite quote is "One day at a time."

DIANE RANGER is founder and president of Colorescience and Body Chemistry Manufacturing, Inc. Diane has been in the cosmetics industry for more than twenty years. She developed the concept of mineral makeup, hundreds of aromatherapy and body-care products, and helped pioneer the concept of specialty body-care stores. Diane founded

Body Chemistry in 1990 to consult with others developing body-care stores and promote private label aromatherapy body-care lines.

CAROL RAVEN is a liberated mom with two grown sons, who loves her husband, Rob, her friends, her church, and herself. Thus far, falling in love with herself is her greatest achievement. She can be contacted at carol@cains.com.

NAOMI RHODE, RDH, CSP, CPAE Speaker Hall of Fame, is an inspirational speaker for healthcare and corporate America. She and her husband, Jim, cofounded SmartPractice, a marketing company. They are the parents of three, and grandparents of twelve. Naomi can be contacted at nrhode@smarthealth.com or 602-225-9090, extension 214.

RICHARD "ROBBY" ROBINSON, AIFD, is a freelance floral designer with twenty-five years' experience. He specializes in silk and preserved designs. Robby is a panel designer and conducts educational workshops and floral programs. He was inducted into the American Institute of Floral Designers in 1996 and is presently a member of the board of the Southern Chapter of AIFD. Robby is active in his local and state florist associations. For more information contact him at 964 East Burgess Road, Pensacola, FL, 32504-7004; 850-477-6700.

DEBORAH ROSE SAPP is the team coordinator registered nurse for a busy eight-bed intensive care unit. She resides in Pikeville, Tennessee, near beautiful Fall Creek Falls State Park.

MARY KOLADA SCOTT lives in Ventura, California, with her husband, Don. Her poems, short stories, articles, and photographs have been published in more than seventy magazines, newspapers, and anthologies. A longer version of this essay originally appeared in the *Ventura County Star* newspaper. Now that her great-grandmother's quilt is finished, Mary expresses her art through watercolor painting. She can be reached at mscott52@earthlink.net.

MARY LOUISE SMITH fell in love with quilting after viewing a Japanese quilt exhibition in 1990. She opted for early retirement in 1994 from international bank management and is planning to embark on a quilting odyssey to explore the art of quilt making. Contact her at MARYLOUISESMITH@webtv.net.

Visit her Web site at http://community-2. webtv.net/MARYLOUISESMITH/MARY LOUISESMITH.

Reneé Sparks is a professional craft designer, author, and television producer living in Atlanta, Georgia. She credits her career choice to all the wonderful women in her family who surrounded her with their amazing creativity.

June Steward divided her time growing up between the farm and the city due to the economic conditions of the Great Depression. She and her husband, Ward, are the proud parents of three children, grandparents of ten, and great-grandparents of two.

Suzann Thompson is an artist, designer, and writer specializing in knitting, crochet, and polymer clay. She teaches workshops internationally and is the author of *Polymer Clay for Everyone* (Rockport Publishers, Inc., 2001). Contact her at suzannt@easynet. co.uk. Though they are native Texans, Suzann, her family, and her dogs enjoy cool weather living in Sheffield, England.

Lynette Turner has been deeply involved

in crafts and sewing throughout her life. As she entered into the world of quilting, she felt at home with other quilters, finding them to be loving, thoughtful, caring, helpful, and deeply devoted to their families. As an expression of love she spends many hours quilting for her family. Her husband, Bill, is so supportive of her quilting that he pushes the cart when she is shopping for fabric and cooks the meals when she is focused on a quilting project.

LIZ WADE has been married to her husband, John, for thirty-seven years. She is the mother of three and grandmother of six. Liz is an environmentalist, retired personal computer teacher at Westinghouse Elevator, and a perpetual quilter.

FRANKIE WOLGAMOTT lives in East Tennessee and was raised in the era when quilt making was a necessity more than a hobby. She has three children, nine grandchildren, and five great-grandchildren. She enjoys reading, quilt piecing, teaching Sunday school, and volunteering for hospice care.

MARCI XENIAS is a wife, mother, and innkeeper of Brooke Mansion Victorian Inn. She enjoys collecting quilts, cups, and saucers, and attending auctions. Her grandparents taught her to care for and enjoy quilts at a very young age. Visit www.brookemansion.com.

JUDITH "JUDIE" ALLEN ZINN is a former administrative secretary who lives in Omaha, Nebraska, and teaches appliqué and hand quilting. She is so busy now, she wonders how she ever had time to work. She can be reached at Zinniadesign@msn.com.

Contributor Earned Designations

AIFD

The American Institute of Floral Designers is the floral industry's leading nonprofit organization committed to establishing and maintaining higher standards in professional floral design. With nearly one thousand members worldwide, AIFD and its members are in the forefront of the industry in presenting educational and design programs. Membership in AIFD is selective. To be accepted, a candidate must fulfill rigid qualifications and demonstrate advanced professional ability. Applicants must successfully complete a two-part process in which they prove their design abilities, first through a portfolio of photographs, and then through an actual on-site design.

CCD

Certified Craft Designer is an earned designation from the Society of Craft Designers, which promotes the professional excellence of its members through educational opportunities and forums for career growth within the craft design industry. It was founded in 1975 as a professional organization for those who believe that quality craft design is the basis of a strong and viable craft industry. It is the only membership organization exclusively serving those who design for the consumer craft industry. They can be contacted at: P.O. Box 3388, Zanesville, OH 43702-3388; 740-452-4541; fax 740-452-2552.

CDE

Certified Death Educator from the Association for Death Education and Counseling, which is a multidisciplinary professional organization dedicated to promoting excellence in death education, bereavement counseling, and care of the dying. Based on theory and quality research, ADEC provides information, support, and resources to its multicultural membership and, through them, to the public. Visit www.adec.org.

CPAE Speaker Hall of Fame

Established in 1977 by the National Speakers Association, the Council of Peers Award of Excellence (CPAE Speaker Hall of Fame) is a lifetime award for speaking excellence and professionalism given to speakers who have been evaluated by their peers and been judged to have mastered seven categories: material, style, experience, delivery, image, professionalism, and communication.

CMG

Color Marketing Group (CMG), founded in 1962 and based in Alexandria, Virginia, is an international, not-for-profit association of sixteen hundred color designers. Color designers are professionals who enhance the function, salability, and/or quality of a product through their knowledge and appropriate application of color. CMG members forecast color directions one to three years in advance for all industries, manufactured products, and services. These consumer/residential and contract/commercial products include: interior/exterior home, transportation, architectural/building, communications/graphics, fashion, action/recreation, and environments for office, health care, retail, and hospitality/entertainment.

CSP

The Certified Speaking Professional designation, established in 1980 by the National Speakers Association, is the speaking industry's international measure of professional platform skill. In addition to their proven track record of continuing speaking experience and expertise, CSPs are committed to ongoing education, outstanding service, and ethical behavior. The CSP designation is conferred only on those accomplished speakers who have earned it by meeting strict criteria, including: serving at least 100 different clients within a five-year period; presenting at least 250 professional speaking engagements within the same five-year period; and submitting testimonial letters from clients served.

NSA:
The Voice of the Speaking Profession
The National Speakers Association (NSA) is an international association of more than thirty-eight hundred members dedicated to advancing the art and value of experts who speak professionally. For more than twenty-five years NSA has provided resources and education designed to enhance the business acumen and platform performance of professional speakers. Please visit NSA's Web site at www.nsaspeaker.org.

CPD
Certified Professional Demonstrator is an earned designation from the Hobby In-

dustry Association (HIA), a New Jersey–based, international trade association. The association was founded in 1940 and now has more than four thousand member companies. HIA promotes crafts and hobbies nationwide through a number of consumer outreach programs and is a leading craft and hobby resource for the general consumer media. The association has also established a strong presence on the Internet through its three Web sites: the popular consumer Web site, www.i-craft.com, the industry Web site, www.hobby.org; and the media resource, www.chib.com.

CPT

Certified Professional Teacher is an earned designation from the Hobby Industry Association.

M.B.A.	**Master's Degree in Business Administration**
M.S.	**Master's in Science**
R.N.	**Registered Nurse**
RDH	**Registered Dental Hygienist**

Kathy Lamancusa likes making a difference in people's lives through ideas and inspiration. She shares new perspectives and adds creative sparks of energy in her work as a professional speaker, author, television host, and media personality. Kathy is also proud to be a mother, wife, quilter, floral designer, and gardener.

She speaks internationally to thousands each year about a wide variety of motivational and business topics. The focus of her motivational presentations includes: understanding current lifestyle, design, and color trends; establishing family traditions and values; balancing life through gardening and quilting principles; nurturing relationships and connections; celebrating the experiences of life; overcoming challenges; as well as enhancing and fostering creativity. She often incorporates quilts and flowers into her presentations. Kathy also speaks to business audiences about current trend forces, visual merchandising, and promotion.

Kathy has written more than thirty-six instructional books and produced fifty flower-arranging and wedding-floral-design instructional videos that are sold internationally. More than 1.6 million of Kathy's books have been sold.

Her television show, *Kathy Lamancusa's At Home with Flowers*, has aired on PBS stations around the United States. Kathy has also appeared as a guest on shows that air on Home & Garden Television, the Discovery Channel, the Learning Channel, TNN, CBN, CNN, and the four major networks. Recently she was a guest on *Oprah*.

She is a freelance writer and editor who works with international trade and consumer magazines providing editorial direction, designs, and articles on lifestyle and color trends. Kathy is the founding editor of *Quilts Are Forever*, a magazine published by Primedia Publications.

Kathy lives with her husband, Joe, in North Canton, Ohio. When not traveling, she enjoys being at home, studying the stars from the center of her hot tub, reading with a hot cup of tea, and walking through the garden. Her two sons, Joe and Jim, are young adults who are studying and traveling the world. Her favorite flowers include lilacs and daisies.

SHARE THE IMPACT OF QUILTS

Quilts speak to us with a language uniquely their own. They comfort us, help us preserve memories, and provide us with a means of sharing with others in ways that touch the heart and soul. I would love to hear your special story. I am planning future books using a similar format, which will feature stories that illustrate the profound effect quilts have on all aspects of our lives.

I am seeking more heartwarming stories, reflections, and memories of up to three pages in length to include in these volumes. I am also very interested in including little-known information about the care and handling of quilts, as well as tried-and-true quilting tips and techniques.

I invite you to join me in sharing the profound message of quilts by sending your stories and information for special consideration. If selected for inclusion, you will be listed as a contributor and may include a biographical paragraph. Send your submissions to:

Creative Directions, Inc.
Quilt Memories
8755 Cleveland Avenue
North Canton, OH 44720

You can submit by e-mail to: editor@ lamancusa.com.

SHARE THE IMPACT OF FLOWERS

Is there a time in your life when flowers brought you joy, gave you a hug, or helped you send a message of hope, love, friendship, or celebration? I would love to hear your special story. I am planning future books using a similar format, which will feature stories that illustrate the profound effect flowers have on life, families, celebrations, love, romance, passion, and sorrow.

I am seeking heartwarming stories, reflections, and memories of up to three pages in length to include in these volumes. I am also very interested in including little-known information about the care and handling of flowers, tips for surrounding yourself with flowers, and garden advice.

I invite you to join me in these future projects by sending your stories and information for special consideration. If selected for inclusion, you will be listed as a contributor and may include a biographical paragraph. Send your submissions to:

Creative Directions, Inc.
Floral Memories
8755 Cleveland Avenue
North Canton, OH 44720

You can submit by e-mail to: editor@lamancusa.com.

"QUILTS ARE FOREVER"
E-MAIL NEWSLETTER

If you want to be touched by more stories, memories, tips, and ideas related to quilting, subscribe to our *free* e-mail newsletter "Quilts Are Forever." Each week you will receive a snippet of quilting information or short story about quilts directly on your desktop to get you ready for your weekend!

To enroll, send a "subscribe to Quilts Are Forever" message to info@lamancusa.com.

"FRIDAY'S FLOWERS"
E-MAIL NEWSLETTER

If you want to be touched by stories, memories, tips, and ideas related to flowers, subscribe to our *free* e-mail newsletter "Friday's Flowers." Each Friday you will receive a snippet of floral information or short story about flowers directly on your desktop to get you ready for your weekend!

To enroll, send a "subscribe to Friday's Flowers" message to info@lamancusa.com.

EXPERIENCE KATHY IN A LIVE PRESENTATION

Kathy Lamancusa speaks to audiences around the world. She is familiar to many because of her television and media appearances, her magazine columns, and her 1.6 million books in print. Her warm, energetic presentation style is inspirational as it motivates audiences to appreciate life more fully.

No doubt about it, life is made up of occasions for rejoicing and trials that challenge us. Kathy will inspire your group members to overcome those challenges and find special moments to celebrate in order to lead a full and balanced life.

Topics of her various presentations include:

Establishing family traditions and values
Nurturing relationships and connections
Appreciating celebrations and
*   overcoming challenges*
Nurturing and enhancing creativity

Her content-rich presentations are exhilarating, results oriented, and highly inspirational. With commonsense wisdom and contagious humor, Kathy offers specific how-to's and action plans that offer hope and encouragement. Her experiences and advice connect with audiences of all ages and backgrounds.

Kathy customizes each keynote, breakout, workshop, or spouse program, incorporating the information that will be most appropriate to the needs of the audience.

For more information on booking Kathy to speak to your group, visit her Web site at www.lamancusa.com or call 330-494-7224.